1984

Change and Tradition
in the
American Small Town

Small Towns Series
Michael Fazio, General Editor

Center for Small Town Research and Design
Mississippi State University

Change and Tradition
in the
American Small Town

Edited by
ROBERT CRAYCROFT
and
MICHAEL FAZIO

UNIVERSITY PRESS OF MISSISSIPPI
Jackson

Library of Congress Cataloging in Publication Data

Main entry under title:

Change and tradition in the American small town.

(Small towns series)
Papers presented at a symposium, hosted by the
Center for Small Town Research and Design at Mississippi
State University.
   1. Cities and towns—United States—Congresses.
2. United States—Social conditions—1980–   —Con-
gresses.   3. City planning—United States—Congresses.
I. Craycroft, Robert. II. Fazio, Michael. III. Missis-
sippi State University. Center for Small Town Research
and Design. IV. Series.
HT123.C46   1983   307.7′62′0973   83-14638
ISBN 0-87805-194-5

Contents

Preface

Because of its setting amidst the many small towns of Mississippi, the School of Architecture at Mississippi State University has assumed as one of its missions addressing the problems faced by the American small town. In 1976 the School formed its Center for Small Town Research and Design as a mechanism for carrying out pertinent research and service activities. In 1982 the School added a related academic component, a new graduate program in small town design—a program which is unique in the nation.

From the beginning, a primary objective of both the Center and the graduate program has been the creation and dissemination of knowledge, an objective of special significance within a field of study that is only now emerging as an identifiable discipline. As scholarship of quality began to be produced, the need became apparent to make the results available to as many of those as possible whom it could benefit. Consequently the Small Towns Series published by the University Press of Mississippi has been initiated.

The Small Towns Series will include the proceedings of each year's Chautauqua in Mississippi, the Center's national symposium on small towns, as well as other scholarly books in the field. Under consideration for publication as part of this series is the reissue of two theoretical and methodological works previously produced at the Center: *The Small Town as an Art Object* and *The Small Town Design Book*.

The first Chautauqua, "Order and Image in the American Small Town," was held in 1980 and the results have appeared under that title. This event was followed in 1981 by "Change and Tradition in the American Small Town," which produced the materials for the present volume. The third Chautauqua, "Research and Design in the American Small Town", was held in 1982, and the proceedings are being prepared for publication. A fourth Chautauqua, "The History of the Small Town" will occur in the fall of 1983.

In the first volume, *Order and Image,* the physical entity of the small town and the place that it occupies in our consciousness were discussed. And now in *Change and Tradition* a dialogue about the small town's past and future is presented. Together these papers explore the issues pertinent to the present status of the American Small Town; and this is the logical first step in planning for the future. As volumes are added to the Small Towns Series, an ever clearer impression will emerge of one of our most valuable, and insufficiently appreciated resources, the American small town.

Michael W. Fazio

Introduction

America's small towns have reached a critical juncture. The same forces confronting the nation as a whole—shifting population patterns, diminishing natural resources, post-industrial economics, and electronic communication networks—signal fundamental changes for them.

Social, political, cultural and economic values must be reconsidered as these changes occur. Decisions that are being made now, in small towns and about small towns, will affect the quality of life there for a generation or more. These decisions must be based on an informed understanding of emerging trends, rather than on out-moded perceptions and misconceptions, if America's small towns are to remain "good places to live."

This newest step in the evolution of the small town must involve a dialogue between the inertia of tradition and the dynamics of change. Many traditional ways of seeing things, doing things, and feeling about things will be in a state of flux. At the same time, traditional institutions and values will play a role in ameliorating the unsettling results of change itself. *Change and Tradition in the American Small Town* examines this dialogue in nine papers selected from the second Chautauqua in Mississippi symposium, hosted by the Center for Small Town Research and Design at Mississippi State University.

If we accept the thesis that form and design are meaningful only to the extent that they reflect, accommodate, and enhance social and cultural realities and aspirations, then we must develop an understanding of the broader context of the small town. A small town, however, cannot be defined as a single reality. Like the characters of William Faulkner's novels, it consists of a multiplicity of descriptions from a variety of perspectives—each accurate yet incomplete. Only by bringing them together can we begin to form a whole and true picture of the subject. This volume brings together essays by a diverse group of humanities and social science scholars to present views of the subject from the vantage point of their respective disciplines.

Perhaps, however, the greater significance of this volume lies beyond the sum of its individual articles (not dissimilar articles may be found in other scholarly and professional journals). Like the symposium, it achieves its stature through its three-dimensionality. The participants became both teacher and students as they stepped beyond the often narrow constraints of their own fields to engage in this dialogue. Professional jargon was replaced by lucid discussion as they exchanged thoughts with those from other disciplines and with the citizens of small towns who attended the Chautauqua. The result is a work that is both informative and accessible.

Change and Tradition in the American Small Town has, since its inception, been intended for a broad audience. Scholars who specialize in small town studies will find articles of interest from their own and allied disciplines. This work presents information upon which design professionals can base their decisions. The citizens of small towns will discover insights that can help them better understand the circumstances in which they are living.

Richard Lingeman, the author of *Small Town America*, begins the discussion in his essay "The Recent Past; The Near Future" by relating America's relationships with the small town to the Broadway musical, *Brigadoon*. Our changing view of the small town evolves, disappears, and reappears in cycles with a persistence that reflects our view of ourselves as individuals and as a nation.

J. B. Jackson suggests that new town forms are evolving (especially in the Southwest and the West and on the perimeters of more traditional towns) that demand our attention. As a landscape historian and longtime observer of the American landscape, he is well qualified to ask that we confer the same legitimacy on new forms as extensions of new life-styles) that we confer on traditional forms.

Robert Tournier, a sociologist, examines the impact that the new urban immigrants will have on small towns. He concludes that neither the newcomers nor the original inhabitants will remain unchanged: each will assimilate the values of the other.

Richard Adicks and Michael Dean, both literary scholars, view the small town through the writings of American authors. The former discusses the small town as a storehouse of inspiration for authors, while the latter presents six books about Mississippi small towns during the turbulent decade of integration. Dean discusses these as chronicles of the demands posed by both change and tradition; he concludes that we need both.

Raymond Coward, a sociologist, examines family life in rural communities for the effects of the demographic trends first documented in the 1980 Census. He presents the concepts of persistence, change, and diversity as collectively capturing the essence of the trends that are converging on family life in small towns today.

David Szczerbacki outlines the changing circumstances of rural communities from an economist's point of view. He discusses the circumstances that shape government policymaker's decisions together with examples that illustrate the process, and he examines the critical issues posed by a reduced federal presence.

Two psychologists, James Brown and Dan Hays, conclude this volume with articles that probe the relationship between man and the small town environment. Brown asks that designers be more cognizant of the relationship between form and behavior, while Hays discusses the small town as a symbol system that conveys important cultural and functional information.

This work stands only as a tentative first step in the necessary interdisciplinary inquiry into the current and emerging realities of American's small towns. That they will undergo dramatic change is clear; the effects are only beginning to manifest themselves. Scholars and professionals must continue to probe for answers to questions that are not yet fully formed and to engage in dialogue with small town advocates from other fields.

Robert Craycroft

Change and Tradition
in the
American Small Town

The Small Town in America:
The Recent Past; The Near Future

RICHARD LINGEMAN

Like Brigadoon in the Broadway musical, small town-America vanishes and reappears in cycles. In Brigadoon, time stood still; American small towns have changed and evolved. Yet there are persisting myths of the American small town that, like Brigadoon, change hardly at all.

This is the small town of memory, the small town that is preserved in the amber of literature and popular culture. Actually, there are several, contrasting images of the small town. There is the stable, conservative, white-picket-fence, corner-store, Norman Rockwell place, where the folks are folksier, the solid middle-class virtues middle-classier, and old-fashioned patriotism stirs in every breast. Then there is the darker view—of a pokey, dull, strait-laced sort of Peyton Place, teeming with secret vices that everybody in town is gossiping about—or even a violent and sinister view, as in the towns of Shirley Jackson's "The Lottery," Ring Lardner's "Haircut" or movies like *Bad Day at Black Rock*. A third view drips with urban condescension and portrays small-town people as quaint, rather innocent but staunch, hard-working folk, who are just not quite with it.

But the small-town myth exists and persists at a deeper stratum of American culture: the small town makes up our image of community. As James Oliver Robertson writes in his book *American Myth, American Reality:*

> For Americans who are bewildered, bruised, or defeated by the freedom of competition and loneliness of the modern world, the images of static rural community still offer refuge. At the same time, these images make the rural community a place of stagnation, hypocrisy, and mindless conservatism. . . . the imagery of homogeneity provides a sense of secure, unchallenging rootedness in a society of the uprooted. The stories of hometowns and parents and grandparents all imply that you *can* go home again. Such stories reflect the fantasy that everything

3

at home is always there, unchanging, immortal: they are the dreams of refuge in a changing, mortal world.

Eric Sevareid once described similar feelings rekindled by a visit to his home town in North Dakota: "I loved its memory always: it was, simply, *home*—and *all* of it home, not just the house but all the town. That is why childhood in the small towns is different from childhood in the city. Everything is home." Each of us who grew up in a small town preserves his own Brigadoon. It is a map, animated by remembrance, etched in one's mind, immutable. The childhood town of memory endures, even as one sees the actual town changing over the years, as in stop-action photography.

And so our memories and images of a small-town America out of our rural past mingle with our perceptions of the real small towns all across our nation today, where many of us are *from* and where twenty-five percent of us live. Periodically, the Brigadoon effect occurs, the small town of our myths and our memories and our stereotypes is summoned up, and there is, as now, an exodus from the cities to rural America; there is much talk of "rural renaissance" and "growth pains." History suggests that renewed interest in the small town comes in times of social upheaval.

Such was the case around the turn of the century, when, amid rapid industrialization and urbanization, small towns achieved their apotheosis in American life. In 1890, seventy percent of all Americans lived in rural regions or small towns of less than 2,500 people. But a rush to the cities had begun. The popular literature and magazines of the day preached the success gospel according to Horatio Alger, exhorting young men to go to the city and make their fortunes. Thousands of young men—50,000 a year to Chicago alone—heeded the call. Their departures from small towns everywhere were evoked in literature. George Willard, the hero of Sherwood Anderson's *Winesburg, Ohio*, climbs aboard the train that will take him to the city and forgets to look back until it is too late: "The town of Winesburg has disappeared and his life there has become but a background on which to paint the dreams of his manhood."

And young women left too—like Carrie Meeber, heroine of Theodore Dreiser's *Sister Carrie:* "A gush of tears at her mother's farewell kiss, . . . a pathetic sigh as the familiar green environs of the village passed in review, and the threads which bound her so lightly to girlhood and home were irretrievably broken." Theodore's brother, Paul Dresser, a famous popular song writer during the eighties and nineties, wrote a song called "She Went to the City." Paul evoked the gray-haired parents back in the home town:

She went to the city, 'twas all they could say,
She went to the city, far, far away,
She grew kind o' restless and wanted to go,
Said she'd be back in a few weeks or so,
She went to the city with a tear in her eye,
But she never returned.

So many George Willards and Carrie Meebers "went to the city" that people began to worry that the countryside and small towns would be depopulated. In 1895 an article entitled "The Doom of the Small Town" described abandonment and decay in the small towns of the Middle West. Fifty years before, New England had experienced a similar wave of concern. The Country Life Movement was founded to study how young men could be lured back to the soil, and in 1908 President Theodore Roosevelt appointed a commission to investigate rural conditions. Popular fiction expressed a counter-revulsion against city life. Booth Tarkington and Zona Gale contrasted the friendliness of the small town with the cruel, amoral, indifferent city. A character in Willa Cather's novel *O, Pioneers*, who has moved to the city, cries out: "Off in the cities there are thousands of rolling stones like me. . . . when one of us dies, they scarcely know where to bury him."

But living conditions on the farms improved, and prosperity returned: World War I boosted farm prices; small towns dependent upon the farmers' trade were thriving. In 1920, a watershed was reached as over half of the American people were found to be living in urban places. But now the small towns became the object of a cultural backlash. Brigadoon reappeared, but this time it was populated by a different sort of folk in books by writers who belonged to a literary movement dubbed (by Carl Van Doren in *The Nation*) "the revolt from the village." These writers rejected the sentimental romance of their literary forebears. They gave us the gallery of hypocrites in Edgar Lee Masters's *Spoon River Anthology*, the repressed grotesques of Sherwood Anderson's *Winesburg*,

and the materialistic boosters of Sinclair Lewis's *Main Street*. The
new wave of intellectuals, typified by H. L. Mencken, hurling
thunderbolts of invective from the ramparts of his *American Mer-
cury*, made the small town a symbol of all they hated in America—
Puritanism, materialism, provincialism, philistinism. As Sinclair
Lewis wrote: "This is America—a town of a few thousand . . . its
Main Street is the continuation of Main Streets everywhere." The
political writer Walter Lippmann saw American politics on the eve
of the 1928 election as a battleground between the opposing forces
of city and country. Rural America, Lippmann wrote, was "in-
spired by the feeling that the clamorous life of the city should not
be acknowledged as the American ideal." He called Prohibition "a
test of strength between social orders. When the Eighteenth
Amendment goes down, the cities will be dominant politically and
socially as they now are economically." The small town had come to
stand for small business-big business Republicanism, opposition to
Reds, radicals, labor unions, foreigners and immigrants, saloons
and liquor, Catholics and Jews, all of which were considered evils
of the big city. The small-town preachers anathematized the cities.
They were Gomorrahs luring innocent youths to ruin with their
bright lights and painted women. But this was a desperate cry of a
dying order, last-ditch propaganda to keep young people at home.
Similar jeremiads had been preached by New England parsons one
hundred years before, when whole towns picked up and moved to
Ohio territory.

The sociologists also discovered the small town. Studies like
Middletown and *Middletown in Transition* by the Lynds; the Yan-
kee City series and *Democracy in Jonesville* by W. Lloyd Warner's
team; *Elmtown's Youth* by A. B. Hollingshead; *Small Town Stuff*
and *Plainville USA*—all appeared during the 1920s and 1930s, all of
them predicated on the idea that the small town was a laboratory
where American life could be dissected and studied. By the 1930s
the small town had almost come to stand for the real America. As
W. Lloyd Warner wrote in 1949, in a preface to *Democracy in
Jonesville:* "The lives of the ten thousand citizens of Jonesville
express the basic values of 180 million Americans." Thornton
Wilder anticipated this view in his 1938 play *Our Town*, which was
set at the turn of the century. In a time of economic collapse and a

looming war in Europe, Wilder's play was a reaffirmation of the old verities embodied in a kind of universalized small town, where nothing ever happens—except the really important things: birth, marriage, death.

Our Town dramatized the fact that the small-town myth was alive and well—and comforting. At one point, Wilder has his stage manager say that the young people of Grover Corners "seem to like it here well enough: 90 percent of 'em graduating from high school settle down right here to live." But of course that was not true— neither in New England, where *Our Town* is set, nor elsewhere. Wilder used myth to soften the hurt of reality. The reality was that the wave of migration from small-town America, which had begun in the last decades of the nineteenth century, continued unabated through the 1950s. Then *another* migration, to suburbia, began in earnest, as city dwellers sought to recapture the small-town dream—while continuing to work in the city. The sociologists and sociological novelists turned their attention to suburbia, and Brigadoon vanished once more.

The most important small-town study of the 1960s reaffirmed the small town's eclipse. *Small Town in Mass Society*, by Vidich and Bensman, purveyed an image of the small town appropriate to its times. This was not new. The Lynds, in the *Middletown* study, had reflected prevailing attitudes toward the small town in the 1920s; their downtown businessmen seem to have stepped from the pages of *Babbitt*. The inhabitants of the upstate New York town studied by Vidich and Bensman were living in a dream world of outmoded creeds. They believed in the old rural values of individualism, self-help, and autonomy, but the authors showed that the town was dependent upon state and federal aid, its politics dominated by a small elite skilled at extracting subsidies from the state, and its small businessmen hard pressed, at the mercy of their big corporate suppliers. Under the authors' pitiless scrutiny, the small town was revealed as an appendage of a mass, urban society, dominated by large institutions of business, government, and mass culture. The town was a last outpost of the old ways; America was becoming monolithically urban.

There was much truth in this picture, of course, but it reflected a bit of the prevailing urban condescension and of the dominant view that America was inexorably becoming a suburban-urban nation, with fewer and fewer family farms, replaced by larger and larger corporate-owned spreads. The country towns that drew their lifeblood from the farmers were fast becoming relics, anachronisms. Caught up in the spirit of the times was the associate director of the U.S. Census Bureau, who predicted in 1971: "Unless there is a large and unprecedented movement out of the metropolitan areas, they will continue to grow and at a rate no less than that of the nation as a whole." America would congeal in the cities, the surburbs, the standard metropolitan areas, while the small towns and rural areas would decline or stagnate.

The associate director was wrong. That serpent in the social scientists' garden, the "unprecedented," struck. By the mid-1970s the demographers were registering blips on their radars of unprecedented sociological objects. The signs of a movement from the metropolitan areas to the rural areas became unmistakable. By 1980, *The New York Times* headlined the official verdict of the Census Bureau: "Rural Areas End Trend, Surpass Cities in Growth." The Census Bureau's preliminary figures for the 1980 census showed that rural counties had increased 15.4 percent in population during the 1970s, compared with a 9.1 percent growth for the city and suburban counties. The increase in population for the United States as a whole was 10.8 percent. Thus, the metropolitan areas, contrary to predictions, had *not* grown as fast as the nation as a whole.

Brigadoon was back. Something was happening out there in the sticks, the boondocks. The most rural counties had gained 8.4 million people during the 1970s. Since people were still moving out of some of these regions, the net gain was actually four million people. But compare that with the 1960s, when the rural areas had a net *loss* of 2.8 million people. For the first time since the initial U.S. census in 1790, with the exception of a couple of years during the depression, the net migration of population was out of the cities, to the countryside.

Once the Census Bureau had confirmed things, the national media sat up and took notice. They heralded as news what demographers had been observing for five years. This, of course, reflects the fact that our census is a decennial one, making a statistical snapshot of a *process* that had been in motion for a long time. But it also shows how slowly the real news breaks through to the national consciousness. Moreover, the press, at best, merely recorded what was going on, unable, it seems, to deal with such questions as causes or implications, falling back finally on a condescending view of small-town activities.

The questions are so complex that any hope for understanding the phenomenon must still lie with the social scientists who have been industriously analyzing it. As a result of their labors, a picture is beginning to emerge, still hazy, parts of it obscure or blurred— but a picture.

Who are the people who are moving out of the cities and metropolitan areas? According to recent studies, a majority of them are white-collar workers, better educated on the average than the rural population. They are not wealthy professionals buying up country properties, nor are they a horde of the urban poor, as some small-town officials seem to fear. A good proportion of them—perhaps a third, in some areas—are older people, retired, or about to retire. But even more of them are young, in their twenties and thirties. Most of them have families. They are not urban Okies; a majority have some kind of tie to the place they move to—relatives or friends, or simply a vacation home. Most of them say they intend to stay.

It is when we come to the question of *why* they moved that a sense of something unique in our history emerges. Most surveys reveal a predominance of those who give as their reason for moving to the small town a desire to improve the quality of their lives; only about a quarter list economic reasons, while fully seventy-five percent cite considerations other than employment. Is this, then, a mass evacuation of blighted cities? The numbers are not large enough to be called "mass." Among the migrants themselves, studies indicate that—except for high taxes—there is no overwhelming dissatisfaction with any particular aspect of urban life. The studies do speak of a *pull* to rural living, but it is hard to pin down the precise "pull" or the "push" that was the main reason for their leaving the cities.

Where do they go to find this coveted quality of life? They go, we are told, to areas "rich in amenities," those that offer room to move around in, and natural beauty. Specifically, eighty percent of them live in or around small towns of less than 5,000 population; most of them, however, choose to live *outside* a town or village. According to the Urban Land Institute, "Nonmetropolitan urban centers have not shared in the revival of nonmetropolitan growth generally. The new growth tends to be diffused to low density small towns and villages and the surrounding new country." As a corollary, the counties with the lowest population density are growing the fastest and attracting the largest number of metropolitan expatriates. The terms "linear suburbs," or "countrified city" have been coined to describe this new landscape—"houses and mobile homes running along roads feeding into population centers."

Those are the facts that have emerged from surveys of metropolitan migrants by the Urban Land Institute and the North Central Regional Center for Rural Development. Because these are sociological surveys, for the most part they lack vividness. A good journalist could brush some of that in, but none has, to my knowledge. Nor have our fiction writers really tackled the subject except obliquely; the linear suburb has yet to have its Sherwood Anderson or Sinclair Lewis or even Grace Metalious. It is still undefined— this new America that is sprouting up out there on the fringes, around the edges, in the legal interstices, on the open land between village and county and township lines. Though some of these areas are large planned developments, many are haphazard growths. They may have shot up along a new sewer line or where a farmer has sold out to a developer near a new road. Some of them are strung like beads around small villages. Some might be called blue-collar suburbia—especially the mobile-home clusters. They satisfy the hunger to own a plot of land at prices working people can still afford.

This then is the new rural sprawl—different from urban sprawl around the edges of a city because the bulk of the growth is taking place in the most sparsely inhabited areas. One random sample of nine rural counties showed that an average of only about a quarter of the total population in each of them lived in urban areas—that is, towns of 2,500 or more—and the rest of the people were scattered in and around villages or out in open country.

Now there is nothing new in this itch of Americans to put distance between themselves and their neighbors. Americans have
been moving to pseudo-rural suburbs with names like Rosebud
Estates and Willow Lane since at least the turn of the century; but
now the urge is to go beyond the suburbs of the 1950s, which have
become too citified, with their crime, their headquarters of large
corporations whose executives are tired of commuting, and the
light industry, the pullulating shopping centers, the traffic jams,
and the crowds.

And so it may simply be that more Americans have acquired the
means to fulfill a yearning to live a small-town or rural life. Polls
have shown as many as eighty percent of Americans expressing the
desire to live and work in a small town—though many want a city
within easy driving distance. By the mid-1970s many of them were
able to fulfill their desire because of interstate highways; cheap gas;
the decentralization of industry with a concomitant increase in
manufacturing jobs in the small towns; deliberate relocation of
federal facilities like military bases to poor, sparsely settled areas;
growth of the recreation and nursing-home industries, with a concomitant growth in service jobs; the proliferation of community
colleges; the energy boom in the Appalachians and the West;
and—at least among retirees—more affluence. A final reason is
cultural—a diminishing of the rural-urban schism. That is, people
do not feel so reluctant to venture out of the city; the "country" is
no longer foreign.

So perhaps we have not had a dramatic flight "*from*" anything or
"*to*" anywhere, but rather a demographic redistribution. We are no
longer, in short, a rural *and* urban-suburban nation, but a *rurban*
nation. Though there is always the chance that the unprecedented
will again happen, or that some specific event like a severe energy
shortage will halt this spreading-out process, it appears that the
trend will continue, or even increase.

Still, if the migration to the countryside continues at its present—or rather mid-1970-rate—by the year 2000 only thirty percent of the population will live in nonmetropolitan areas—which is
less than what it was in 1950. But even if rural growth is relatively
small, the impact on the counties and towns where it is taking place
will be disproportionately large. The "countrified city," in J. C.

Doherty's phrase, is quite likely the city of the future. City planner John Friedmann gives us a picture of it—and still another sobriquet: the "plug-in city." He conjures up this vision of the future American countryscape:

> Farms and forests are interspersed with clusters of urban settlements and centers of productive work. But the land is no longer primeval. In a fundamental way, whether its use is in agriculture or not, it has become urbanized. Architects call it a plug-in city, by which they mean that anywhere within the urban field one can connect his home to an intricate and, for the most part, efficiently managed network of freeways, telephones, radio and television outlets, and electrical energy and water supply systems.

Thus, it appears that the so-called rural renaissance is not an unmixed blessing for the small towns, for the countryside—or for the country. It has created pollution, environmental degradation, disappearing farm land. New people mean the need for new water, sewer and electrical lines, new schools, and new roads. Extra burdens are placed on creaking local governmental structures and a patchwork of overlapping jurisdictions that were not set up to cope with much of the development. Problems are created that are county-wide, but many county governments have neither the desire nor the skills to undertake the necessary planning. For one thing, money must be raised for new services, meaning added burdens for the old residents, whose incomes often are less than those of the newcomers. The boom towns of the West are experiencing serious social problems from a rapid influx of outsiders. Towns desperately expand their services to cope, for example, with the prosperity of a new energy boom—and people wonder what they will do with the new schools after the energy runs out and the workers move on.

Businesses relocating in the small towns create jobs—but many of them are taken by outsiders, while the local people are handed the higher tax bill for necessary new services, not to mention the bill for the tax easements given to the new business to attract it in the first place. So-called footloose industries seeking non-union labor come in—but sometimes move on to find even cheaper labor in Taiwan or South Korea. Conglomerates buy up long-established locally owned businesses, then cut back or close them down when they are no longer considered cost-efficient. Shopping centers mushroom in former corn fields and draw trade away from decaying central business districts of the small towns. Though this plague of woes is not spreading across the land like an epidemic, various of its symptoms are common in many parts of the country.

Certainly the national implications of this social change have not been completely understood by our leaders and opinion-makers. The Carter Administration's policy for the countryside was unsuccessful because it attempted to apply urban solutions to non-urban problems. The Reagan Administration's vow to return power to the local governments raises the question of whether those governments, already hard pressed fiscally, reluctant to raise taxes, and facing new, unprecedented problems caused by the new migration, can do the job. Can they begin to engage in the kinds of planning necessary to preserve those amenities that drew people to their towns and villages and counties in the first place?

A whole new infrastructure of services in the countryside will be needed at a time when older areas are seeking to stem decay. A battle over the allocation of resources is looming, and it will be fought out in Washington and the state capitals. And what does the new migration imply about our national character? Are we searching for a renewal of ties with the land, for face-to-face community? Or, on the the contrary, are we becoming an ever more rootless, mass society—a plug-in society? Are we, as one author of a report issued by President Carter's Urban Commission indicated, being "decanted" from cities as the national economy dictates, moveable parts in that economy? If so, do we have no other choice?

Even though we live in what Lester Thurow calls a "zero-sum society," I believe we *do* have choices. We need not engage in urban triage and let the most seriously wounded places die. By the same token, we must not let the rural areas lose the natural assets that made them magnets to disaffected urbanites in the first place.

Nowhere is the sense of place more important than in the South. Mississippian William Faulkner's novels were steeped in a sense of place. Faulkner created his own place, a mythical county called Yoknapatawpha, out of the land and people he knew in and around his own Oxford. This county, he said, had a story: a "chronicle which was a whole land in miniature, which multiplied and com-

pounded was the entire South." For him place was inextricable
from history and ancestral links going back through time.

But running against this sense of place, the longing for roots, is a
trend toward *"placelessness."* A sense of a newer America was
expressed by a contemporary writer, William Gass, in his story,
"In the Heart of the Heart of the Country." "The Midwest," Gass
wrote—for which you could easily substitute "America"—"The
Midwest. A dissonance of parts and people, we are a consonance of
towns. Like a man grown fat in everything but heart, we over
labor: our outlook never really urban, never rural either, we en-
large and linger at the same time, as Alice both changed and remained in her story."

In *Through the Looking-Glass* Lewis Carroll's Alice at one point
found herself having to run twice as fast just to remain in one place.
Small towns chasing growth and "progress" may find themselves
doing that these days. But they must not be so overwhelmed by
change or "progress" that the land, rural America, is lost. Faulkner
had a feeling for the land. He wrote of "This land, this South, for
which God has done so much, with woods for game and streams for
fish and deep rich soil for seed and lush springs to sprout it and
long summers to mature it and serene falls to harvest it and short
mild winters for men and animals." But Faulkner saw what was
happening, for he also wrote of ". . . this land which man has
deswamped and denuded and derivered in two generations. . . ."

We must continue to preserve this land, rather than subdivide
the remnants whenever someone bids highest dollar. And we must
also preserve our small towns—their good old buildings, their
Main Streets and central business districts, their courthouses—
even their abandoned railroad stations, by converting them to art
galleries or farmers' markets. But we should preserve them as
places and the towns as *communities*.

At the outset, I mentioned the durability of the small-town myth
in our national memory, and how it had come to stand for community. We can, of course, question the validity and relevance of the
small-town myth, based as it is on a bygone country town, now
bathed in hazy illusions. We can worry about an "environmental-
ism" that serves only wealthy property owners, a "preservation"
that bars "undesirables." Nonetheless, the myth has its foundations

in our unique history—towns were anchors in our westward tide. The myth owes its durability to a need that persists.

Small towns today have many of the problems of the city. Yes, they can be stultifying, lonely, dead little places, as Sherwood Anderson showed in his *Winesburg, Ohio* stories. But Anderson also wrote—remembering his own hometown of Clyde, Ohio— about the tradition of community, a tradition that can be traced back to the early Puritan settlers in New England. To Sherwood Anderson, there was an "invisible roof" of community over the little pre-industrial towns of the Middle West, and he feared it would be swept away in the onrush of industrialization. What he wrote about those little Ohio towns expresses a yearning that has not died out:

> And the people who lived in the towns were to each other like members of a great family. . . . a kind of invisible roof, beneath which everyone lived, spread itself over each town. Beneath the roof boys and girls were born, grew up, quarreled, fought and formed friendships with their fellows, were introduced into the mysteries of love, married and became the fathers and mothers of children, grew old, sickened, and died. Within the invisible circle and under the great roof everyone knew his neighbor and was known to him. Strangers did not come and go swiftly and mysteriously, and there was no constant and confusing fear of machinery and of new projects afoot. For the moment mankind seemed about to take the time to understand itself.

We must not lose that ideal of community; it is like a twin star to our individualism, our rootlessness, our freedom, our mobility and openness to change. We may be in danger of losing it. In 1980, the National Advisory Council on Economic Opportunity issued one of those many reports that advisory commissions are wont to issue. But some words in the report seem especially relevant when we are concerned with aimless violence and when fiscal constraints are shrinking social services. I quote *The New York Times:* "In a discussion of the relationship between poverty and shifting national values, the report said that the 'erosion of community and religious ties as well as the increasing uniformity of national life has paralleled the rise of a national pattern of brutal social inequality.'"

The traditional values of the small town stand squarely in contrast to an emerging mass, uniform, plug-in society. Egalitarianism, grass-roots government, active involvement with place, trust, face-to-face relations over a period of time with one's neighbors and townsmen, human scale, the personal, rather than the impersonal—these are some of the values we should think about preserving along with the material dimensions of small towns. Call it quality of life, or whatever, more and more people *are* seeking these things, and I think the small towns could be in the forefront of this movement. If they should be, it would be a first—those conservative, pokey, backwater small-towns in the avant garde of a new America.

Country Town

JOHN B. JACKSON

In the seventeenth century, when Englishmen began coming to the New World to live, people distinguished between what was a town and what was a city not on the basis of size or density or wealth, but on the basis of the role that each kind of settlement played. A city was thought of as the seat of authority. It was the place where the government had its headquarters, the place where the church was centered, the place where society was organized in a hierarchy of power and position. The city was the symbol of the commonwealth, its dignity and permanence. That was one reason why Governor Winthrop hoped that the Puritan colony would become "a city upon a hill."

Yet Boston was established not as a city but as a town. A town was where people lived. It was a collection of farms or dwellings and it was more or less the same as a parish. A New England town, as we all know, meant a sizeable piece of land, more or less thirty-six square miles, and it could include not only many farms and homesteads but several small villages. In Western Massachusetts you can see a sign which says: "Town of Montague. Village Limits of Montague City."

In Virginia, where there were never many villages and where people lived at some distance from each other, the word *city* was used more often to indicate any settlement, no matter its size, which was a center of administration. At the very beginning the colonists decided there would be four or five cities: Henrico City, Elizabeth City, Jamestown, and eventually, of course, Williamsburg. But, instead of speaking of "the city *of* Jamestown," for example, they talked about "the city *at* Jamestown," "the city *at* Enrico." There is something bewildering about place names in the United States, especially in the South: in Virginia there is a small place called Elizabeth City County Courthouse—which is almost as hard to interpret as the street name in Baltimore: Charles Street Avenue Boulevard. I imagine a linguist would deduce that the way we use the word *city* is indicative of a change in the way we define the word. For instance, it has now become very common to find businesses called Car Wash City, Surplus City, Buick City. What do we mean by *City?* As far as I can see, it means a place where there is a concentration of some type of service or some type of goods.

Perhaps that is how we are beginning to define the city itself: a place where there is an unusual concentration of goods and services. The great difference between the seventeenth-century concept of what a city was and this current concept suggests that it is perhaps time to redefine *town*.

I think we all agree that there is a definite type of small community with special social and cultural and economic characteristics, but size has really very little to do with the definition of *town*. I find myself thinking less of *small* town than of *country* town. The country towns are the ones I especially like and which I have explored over the last thirty years. My interests are those of the average tourist, one who happens to be also a landscape historian, who likes to see how the forms of towns, the spatial relationships differ from one part of the United States to another. I have come to prefer the country towns of the Midwest and the South, and I would tentatively define the country town as a place which has close ties with the nearby countryside, which is the characteristic of the Southern version.

Very early in its history, Tidewater Virginia, was divided into counties. They were small and very sparsely populated, but each county had to have a courthouse. Where was the best place to put it? The solution was to place it as near the center of the county as possible, or perhaps at an important crossroads. So the early settlers, without realizing what they were doing, created one of the most unusual and most charming features of the colonial landscape: the formal brick courthouse, surrounded by lawn and trees, way out in the empty countryside. Virginians, even in those days, were a very gregarious, social-minded people; they lived far apart and it was not easy to pay calls on neighbors when there were rivers and marshes to cross. The monthly sessions of the county court, the yearly elections, and the paying of taxes served as reasons for everyone's coming together at the courthouse. Men and women

and children, tired of their lonely homes and tired of hoeing to-
bacco, gathered from all around the county to have a holiday and
see friends. They came in wagons or on horseback or on foot—
hunters, backwoodsmen, small farmers, and rich plantation
owners. They paid their debts, sold or bought anything from
shovels to pieces of land, and when there was an election under-
way, they listened to the speeches and drank the free liquor which
the candidates handed out.

No wonder the common people of Colonial Virginia loved their
courthouse just as much as New Englanders loved their church.
But what made the courthouse a valuable institution, it seems to
me, was not only that it brought people together and gave them a
good time but also that it was a political institution. It was where
people debated issues and discussed county affairs. The courthouse
was in that sense the local equivalent of a city in the classical
meaning of the word: *civitas*, a collection of citizens.

But there is one thing about this courthouse place of assembly
that we should not forget: as a kind of city it too had its hierarchy. It
had people who could not vote and those who could. Those who
held office and those who did not. It had its group of rich and
powerful men, and its majority of poor and ignorant people. And
each group, each class knew where it belonged in the social order.
As I suggested earlier, this was at one time an essential characteristic of a city. It was also characteristic of the courthouse public, for
all its friendliness and informality.

The Virginians were so fond of their courthouses and of their
counties that when they started to move over the mountains into
what is now Kentucky and Tennessee, they took the courthouse
with them, and very soon the new landscape had its brand new
counties and its log-cabin temporary courthouses. But it was not
long before the new settlers, and the land speculators among them,
began laying out towns to serve as centers. Farmers were raising
commercial crops and they needed markets not too far away. The
sale of new land and the unending flow of newcomers to the region
demanded the services of lawyers and surveyors and the offices of
the land bureau. There was a need for teachers and clergymen.
And in many of the new-planned towns, a courthouse was a vital
element.

There developed the practice of laying out new towns meant to be county seats. The procedure was simple enough. The real-estate operators and speculators set aside a block of land in the center of the new town and often donated it to the community as a site for a courthouse. Eventually a typical Southern courthouse town evolved.

A wonderfully complete study of courthouse towns was made several years ago by E. T. Price, who is professor of geography at the University of Oregon. There are more than three thousand counties in the United States, each with its county seat and its courthouse, and Professor Price has visited them all. There are several different kinds of courthouse squares. In Pennsylvania and Ohio and West Virginia and Kentucky there are courthouses located at the intersection of two streets; these are known as Philadelphia or Lancaster courthouse squares, after the two earliest eighteenth-century examples. The Southern type of square is much simpler. It is merely one block in the center of a town composed of uniform rectangular blocks. This was thought to be the logical place for a building, in the very center. But it took time to formulate the plan, and the first county seat where the court-house was deliberately located on a block by itself in or near the center of town was a small place in southwestern Tennessee called Shelbyville. This was in 1819.

How the Shelbyville plan spread we do not know; but in a few decades courthouse squares of this sort appeared as far north as Iowa and Missouri, as far east as South Carolina, and as far south as Texas, where in fact you find the most beautiful examples. Anyone who has traveled through the Upper South or the Gulf South will be familiar with these courthouse towns. The courthouse itself dominates its surroundings with a tower or dome and an elaborate stone or brick facade, and is often an extraordinary specimen of nineteenth-century public architecture. (Several books about these buildings have recently appeared.) At one time I regretted the destruction of any one of these monuments and its replacement by a courthouse of a more modern style, but I have learned to accept the replacements. Even those dating from twenty or ten years ago try to be monumental, and in a generation or so will be respectfully studied by architectural historians.

I have seen a great many of these courthouses, though nothing
like as many as Professor Price. My picture of them is not unusual:
I see them as having played much the same social and political role
as did those courthouses in Virginia, though to be sure the setting
is urban and more complicated. Generally speaking, I would say
the smaller the town the more effective was the courthouse as a
gathering place. It was always an important element in downtown
activities. The square around it was occupied by small, locally
owned retail stores; the movie theater was there; the small hotel
was there, and so were the barbershop and the cafe or restaurant
where the town businessmen ate their lunch; and of course there
was always a corner bank with a clock and thermometer. Idle men,
many of them old, sat on the courthouse steps or on benches under
the shade of trees. I somehow do not think of it as a space where
there were many women. There were monuments on the lawn
surrounding the building. No matter how shabby or how unsightly
it might have been, architecturally speaking, the courthouse dominated its surroundings. I know of no other urban composition anywhere in the United States that was so picturesque, so dignified
and in general so satisfactory.

But I must say once again what I said about the Virginia courthouse: the importance of the nineteenth-century courthouse was
not that it was simply a congenial gathering place. It was also a
political institution for producing citizens. A courthouse was, of
course, very useful to the economy of the town. It brought people
in from the surrounding countryside on legal or tax matters, it
provided space for a weekly market, and it concentrated the retail
business within a compact area. But more than that it was a place
for discussion, a place for speeches, a place for celebration. It was a
place above all where the social composition of the town was dis-
played: important politicians, important businessmen and lawyers
and social figures went in and out and were watched from a re-
spectful distance. This was the hub, the focal point not only of the
town but of the surrounding landscape.

What I am describing is, of course, a glimpse of the past. So it
may not be inappropriate to quote from a description of a typical
Alabama country town written some seventy-five years ago by Clifton Johnson, an itinerant photographer and the author of several

charming books about his travels in rural America at the turn of the century.

> The town is widestreeted and placid, with a broad public square at its heart, bounded by brick and wooden stores, law offices, etc. These structures are one and two stories high, and are pretty sure to have projecting from their fronts, across the sidewalk, an ample board roof to furnish shade; and between the supports of the roof, on the outside of the walk, is usually a plank seat. The walk is a good deal encumbered with displays of various goods, and here and there are huddles of empty whiskey barrels and other receptacles. The barrels and boxes, in common with the plank seats and sundry doorsteps and benches, are utilized very generally by loungers. The populace like to sit and consider, and they like to take their ease when talking with their friends. . . . A more aristocratic loitering place than any provided by chance or intention as adjuncts of the stores, is a group of chairs at the rear door of the courthouse. Every pleasant day these chairs are brought out into the shadow of the building and the nearby trees, where they are occupied by some of the village worthies for the purpose of mild contemplation and discussion. . . . The business square on which the court-house looks out from its enthroning trees with serene though antiquated dignity is usually very quiet. The town life is not very energetic. A good many of the stores get along without sign boards, and I frequently heard their proprietors whiling away their leisure in the recesses of their shops with a guitar, or cornet, or fiddle. . . . Saturday is, however, an exception. That is market day, and the public ways and hitching places are then crowded with mules and horses, many of them merely saddled, others attached to vehicles . . . ox teams are common, and once in a while a negro drives a single ox harnessed between his cart-shafts.

I remember many such country towns from the early days of my travels. I remember the handsome, spacious residential streets shaded by large trees and bordered by white houses with great porches. Somewhere near the center was often a small sectarian college, a composition of old-fashioned brick buildings, a little down at the heel, perhaps, as if student life were a perpetual vacation and the college endowment little more than a dozen farms out in the country, raising corn or hay and not much else. Down the hill toward the depot in a tangle of vines was the black section of town, and somewhere hardly out of sight was a wide brown river where people were fishing. I remember the good food at the restaurant on the square, the sound of hymn singing coming from

every church on Wednesday night, and above all, the general
sense of completeness, as if the town had achieved its purpose of
producing contented, well-behaved people and had decided not to
grow or change. Not to grow or change means in America to run
the risk of decay and ultimate death: but when did this paralysis set
in? I think it was when the town lost its political role.

That was a generation ago, and that kind of small town was what
I saw in the Old South. But there is another kind of courthouse
town or county seat, probably less familiar, at least to travelers in
the East. I mean the much newer, much less beautiful courthouse
towns that have developed over the last decades and that are still
developing in the High Plains and Rocky Mountain Country.

As you undoubtedly know there are many counties in Texas—to
be exact, 254. Many of them are small. One ranch stretches over
parts of ten counties: the celebrated XIT "Ranch-Ten in Texas."
Furthermore there are many medium-sized counties in western
Kansas, in eastern New Mexico and throughout the High Plains
and the Rockies all the way to the Canadian border. Few of them
have a large population. Until recently they were devoted to
ranching and wheat farming, with most of the inhabitants living
near or at the county seat—a town with perhaps five or six
thousand people. But over the past decade many of these towns
have come to life and a degree of prosperity—thanks, very often, to
the discovery and exploitation of a valuable natural resource like oil
or gas or uranium or coal, or because of a new irrigation project.

I have traveled many times through the High Plains county,
which is a beautiful and spacious landscape, and I have found that
these small towns, unlike many of those in the East, have expanded in a relatively orderly manner and have in some cases
become communities of promise. In many ways they resemble the
traditional county-seat model, but what is interesting about them is
how they have developed a morphology of their own, and even a
way of life of their own in that none of them plays the traditional
role of producing citizens in the old-fashioned sense.

None of them, to be sure, departs from the established American grid layout—except perhaps in the case of a small, prosperous
semi-suburban residential development. The grid, in fact, is much
more conspicuous because the terrain is usually level with few tall

trees. The streets are broader, and only two or three of them bear historical names. East and west they are numbered; north and south they are given letters of the alphabet—or the system is reversed. There are dozens and dozens of identical rectangular blocks bordered, most of them, by neat, rectangular one-story houses each with its bright green lawn and each with a pick-up truck parked in front; and there are rows and rows of small Chinese elms or Russian olives, waving in the incessant wind. In time they will grow into trees of some size, but now they scarcely cast a shadow. It is only in the oldest part of town, down by the depot and beyond the railroad tracks, that you catch a glimpse of what the place was like a half century ago, when it was little more than a village where most men worked for the railroad. There are dilapidated frame houses with large trees and yards full of tricycles and old cars. Almost everywhere you look you can see the immense surrounding rolling landscape. Sometimes there are oil pumps, slowly nodding up and down. There is little color in the view, but when a cloud briefly hides the sun there are brilliant contrasts of light and shadow.

For three or four blocks Main Street is lined with retail business establishments, and the Courthouse Square, a block in the center of town following the old Southern custom, is likewise lined with small, modest one-story buildings: post office, newspaper, one of the several banks, beautician's, men's wear and so on. These are certainly not handsome specimens of architecture, but they are practical. For as we all know, the small American town, even the small American city, can no longer support three- or four-story buildings in the business section. For many reasons, no small business, no office, no agency wants to be up a flight of stairs. One of the depressing sights in the traditional courthouse square is the number of vacant or boarded-up windows in the second and third stories of the old brick buildings. The new towns in the High Plains have managed to avoid this blight. Architects eager to help revitalize the small downtown area could, I think, be more profitably employed in designing—or redesigning—the one-story offices and stores to give them something like style than in trying to preserve or rehabilitate the few two- or three-story buildings which survive.

As for the courthouse itself, it has dignity because of its isolation

and its bulk, and it is in fact the only structure in town with
architectural pretensions. Even so it is modern enough in spirit to
betray the contemporary attitude toward public buildings. It is not
designed to be a palace or a monument as courthouses were a
hundred years ago; it is treated like an office building and so has no
dome or tower and no columns. The open space surrounding it is
planted in grass. There is seldom a statue or a monument or even
an historic marker. Several decades ago a replica of the Statue of
Liberty, five feet high, was given to every town which had done its
share in World War One. What organization was responsible for
this generosity I do not know, but inevitably in the course of years
and because of neglect the statues have deteriorated, sometimes
losing their heads, and I imagine they will soon disappear al-
together. Probably because it offers little shade and is somewhat
isolated from what pedestrian traffic there is, the square does not
seem a popular place for loitering. In brief, the new courthouse, I
would say, has little symbolic value. What stands out on the skyline
of the town are the grain elevators, the screen of the drive-in
movie, and the water tower. After dark there are few bright lights
except for the vapor lights along Main Street and the red-and-
green lights of the string of motels.

Is there indeed in these towns any visible element of the old or
picturesque or inspiring? I think not. There are no recognizable
architectural antiquities, nothing worth preserving and restoring.
The oldest surviving residence of any character dates from perhaps
1910, and it is either a funeral home or in a state of imminent
collapse. In many of these remote, isolated places the important
state highway runs down Main Street. This creates the illusion of
traffic and encourages a certain amount of drive-in business, but
generally speaking these are towns you drive through at 45 m.p.h.;
they interrupt so briefly the experience of empty sunlit space that
you scarcely notice them.

Nevertheless they have features which seem to be effective in
producing, on a modest scale, an illusion of community life and
which I think could be imitated. If the Courthouse Square is not
the most important gathering place there are several substitutes.
These towns, possibly because of the over-generous scale of their
layout, have many vacant spaces which serve as playgrounds and

potential parks. There is usually a poorly maintained rodeo
ground, and the school provides a football field, a baseball diamond
and an informal picnic area. Shopping centers are, to be sure, part
of every American town; but in these Western communities,
where these centers are rarely landscaped and have great expanses
of parking area, the canopies over the fronts of the stores are places
of sociability and even the scene of such popular events as the
arrival of Santa Claus in a helicopter, the oratory of political candidates, and the display of new-model cars. It is in the store windows
that you find all announcements of bake sales, revivals, ballet lessons, and garage sales.

But there is one gathering space in these towns that I think is
without parallel in towns in the older parts of the country. I am
thinking of the strip development along the highway at both ends
of Main Street.

Often the strip is not only ugly and offensive but inefficient as
well; it is its inefficiency and lack of order, I think, that disturbs its
critics and the general public. But we must not overlook the fact
that the strip serves an important function in the American community. It is hardly necessary to point to the role which the automobile plays in our life, and in rural or semi-rural areas our
dependence on the automobile is magnified; we cannot survive
without it. There has to be a place where we can easily go to have
the truck or automobile serviced, where the truck or automobile
can be bought or sold, and where the several aspects of automobile
usage are taken care of. Before we condemn the anarchy of the
strip we should ask ourselves if we would prefer to have it scattered
in fragments throughout our towns and cities. Repair shops, sales
lots, garages can be noisy, smelly, crowded places with much coming and going, and they are places which demand a great deal of
space. Is it not better to have most of these auto-related establishments located on both sides of a wide thoroughfare where there is
already heavy traffic?

The strip is, however, more than an area devoted to the sale and
servicing of trucks and automobiles. In many parts of America
where large-scale technology is invading the countryside, it is fast
becoming the place where specialized equipment is serviced and
sold and where, in consequence, we are likely to find specialized

skills. This is where we see the immense, brightly colored displays of mechanized farm equipment. In regions of mining and drilling and irrigation and large-scale construction this is where we find engineering firms and services. This is where the out-of-town worker or foreman comes to find talent and help in maintaining or repairing the equipment he uses. It is perhaps too much to say that the strip in the rural center is the focus of expertise, but I think it is where we find certain skills and certain products which the town itself does not need. What we see along the strip, more and more, are gatherings of field workers and mechanics and construction foremen. The motels and restaurants are often crowded with men who have come to town in search of help; and motels are even serving as small conference centers, where new ideas, new problems, new solutions in the world of technology are exchanged. I know of no more vital area in the town, and a well-equipped, well-planned, versatile strip is what these new towns depend on to attract outsiders and to maintain contact with the rural economy. Above all, this kind of strip provides good jobs for young people, and for that reason alone every town, if it can, should have vocational-technological classes in its high school.

A further feature of the strip is that it is not only the locus of the automobile economy, not only the technological center but also the place where young people go for pleasure. It was the South, I think, that first discovered the attractions of the strip; it was here that the younger generation first learned to spend its leisure cruising up and down from one drive-in to another. This is a noisy and often extravagant way of passing the evening, but by and large it is as good a form of recreation as we can offer to small-town youth. Is it not really much better than the old-fashioned horse culture of the past? From what we learn of that culture it was thoroughly disreputable and vicious: concentrated in back alleys and in livery stables, dirty, dishonest, and frequented by the lowest element in the population and the object of widespread and probably justified disapproval. This cannot honestly be said of the strip. Eating junk food and showing off may not be a profitable way of passing time, but in the long run it is relatively harmless and it has nothing surreptitious or furtive about it. Those who recommend that the strip as the place of entertainment and of transient accommodations should be separated from the strip as place of work and business have a point. But we need to analyze the strip, its hazards and opportunities, before we undertake to control it or abolish it.

If these small new towns without cultural pretensions and (it should be added) without any clear vision of their future possess any qualities worth emulating I think we should first of all admire their broader streets, their larger lots, their lower density, and their more spacious, more relaxed layout. I think their strip development suggests a better way to organize the industrial aspects of the urban morphology—hitherto of necessity concentrated near the railroad tracks where they have produced slums. A third advantage which these towns in the High Plains have is better housing, a result of the fact that land was once cheap and that in colder or brisker climates houses were sturdily built and were provided with utilities suited to the weather. Moreover, unlike the older towns of the South and East, these newer towns built few houses on a speculative basis for unskilled labor. I am thinking of the remarkable collection of shotgun houses in Greenwood, Mississippi, block after block of them, put up, as I understand it, to accommodate the unskilled labor employed in the cotton industry, and now entirely occupied by blacks. No doubt when they were built they seemed adequate enough—at least to the builders. In the West, however, houses recently built have either been of the pre-fabricated mail-order variety or made of cement block because of the expense of lumber. The current solution to the problem of rapid population growth is the mobile home—or what is often called manufactured housing. This is not a form of dwelling likely to be popular with Easterners. The appeal of the trailer community is not so much visual as it is the better, more spacious quality of domestic life, and the temporary nature of the groups. Instead of becoming an ever-deteriorating slum, the neighborhood composed of mobile homes usually disappears or disintegrates.

Cheap and decent housing has never been abundant in rural or small-town America, but in my part of the country—the Southern Rockies—it has now become a matter of urgency. As many of you know the Rocky Mountain West and the High Plains are expecting over the next decade a population increase at at least 20%. These two or three million people will for the most part be young blue-collar workers, most of them of foreign origin, who will be involved not only in the construction and operation of the new energy projects, but in building the vast infrastructure of roads, towns, dams, airfields, recreation areas and so on. Whatever we may feel about the almost total transformation of what has been an empty and beautiful part of the world, we must face the fact that in a short time twenty or thirty small, industrialized towns are to be created; and they must be planned with perhaps a thirty- or forty-year lifespan in mind.

This can be done. We know how to build on a temporary basis and how to build fast and efficiently. But we must somehow establish a reasonable relationship between the new towns and their desert or wilderness environment. We must not destroy or defile that environment, needless to say, but can we not somehow incorporate in these new landscapes some of the good qualities we have associated with the traditional courthouse town here in the South? I myself can think of many characteristics—social as well as environmental—I would like to see incorporated in the new towns to be built: a kind of self-sufficiency and independence of metropolitan ways, a solidarity and sense of kinship among people, an intimate and affectionate relationship with the immediate rural surroundings and with those who live there, and lastly a respect for local history and its monuments—an awareness of corporate dignity.

On the other hand there are old-fashioned civic traits which are clearly not to be carried over into the future: certain entrenched class and racial distinctions, a dependence on an old-fashioned inefficient agriculture, a feeling of completeness, a disdain for experimentation, and a nostalgic attitude toward a long-vanished past.

In strictly physical terms the new towns will be larger and more populous. Twenty years ago it was generally thought that no country town, no matter how self-contained, could survive without such facilities as a high school, a hospital, a supermarket, a variety of professions and trades. Such a town, it was said, would have to have a population of at least 10,000 in order to support these facilities. (I imagine that that figure should now be at least doubled.) One reason is that the basic relationship between town

and countryside is changing. The surrounding countryside is play-
ing a very different, a more demanding role, encompassing both
the place where much of the active population goes to work—in
construction or processing or mining or in a highly mechanized
form of agriculture—and the place where people go for increasingly popular forms of recreation: fishing, boating, hunting, rock
hunting, camping, and exploring. But even with this radical
change the traditional definition of the small town can still be valid;
a small country town can still be a community where people are
brought together by living near one another, where they freely
work together and celebrate together. It can still be a community
where existence can be made more complete by close and frequent
contact with the rural setting.

Small Towns
at the Crossroads:
Outcome Scenarios in Non-Metropolitan Change

ROBERT E. TOURNIER

Attitudes in our society toward the small town are marvelously schizophrenic. On the one hand, we extol the virtues of small-town America as a reminder of the persistence of a way of life that we regard as nearly utopian. Even those of us who live by choice in metropolitan areas frequently engage in a sort of psychic flight to the top of Walton's Mountain, to look down upon a world far more perfect than that in which we have chosen to live—a world without crime or violence, without noise or pollution, without any of the liabilities of living in cities. It is thus not surprising that while a clear majority of Americans live in urban areas, an even larger majority insist that they would prefer to live in open country or in small towns.[1]

We harbor, on the other hand, some strong suspicions about small-town life, and the characterization of the small town as evil, frightening, clannish, or corrupt is now a fixed stereotype in American mass culture. To a generation reared on a cinema diet of *Bad Day at Black Rock, In the Heat of the Night, Deliverance*, or *Easy Rider*, small towns are dangerous, malevolent places; in the 1960's and 1970's the small towns of the South, in particular, were regularly libeled by media as the last bastions of reactionism in America, as places where segregation and night riders, superstition and ignorance prevailed. I believe that, in part, many of our attitudes toward the small town are a fundamental outgrowth of characteristics of urban life, for one of the ways we have learned to survive in cities is to wall ourselves off, both physically and emotionally, from one another. As we have done so, our attitudes toward interaction have changed, for to extend the hand of friendship in many of our cities is to risk losing one's watch if not one's hand, and interaction with others is seen not as rewarding but as incurring unwanted obligations. To people accustomed to this situation, life in small towns is threatening indeed: people there talk to

31

you and by doing so, fill you with a dread of privacy compromised; people talk to each other, and in doing so raise the specter of a kind of clannishness threatening to those who pride themselves on their independence.

Stereotypes aside, the twentieth century has been the age of the city, and the concerns of social scientists throughout the age have been focused on the city, its problems, and its potential. The city was celebrated as the most visible symbol of the creative genius of our civilization, the setting from which sprang the most dynamic products of our culture. The years after the Second World War did little more than confirm our suspicion that the age of the city was at hand. We began to speak not merely of the city but of what Mumford called megalopolis[2]—huge concentrations of people spreading over hundreds of square miles, dominating politically and economically the regions in which they were spawned.

What of the small towns of America? They and the way of life they represented were seen as inexorably doomed. In 1910, the rural population of our country was about thirty-two million; by 1970, it had fallen to just over nine million. In the late 1950's and early 1960's, only forty percent of those born in rural America still lived in rural America, and there seemed little doubt that this exodus from the countryside to the city would continue.[3] Why the flight? The attractions of city life played a part, of course, but a more fundamental motivation was economic, for changes in agricultural technology created a huge pool of under-utilized labor for which the future was bleak indeed. The young left, as did the educated and the adventurous, and many of our small towns were turned into hollow shells with chronic fiscal crises and rapidly aging populations. Small towns came to be seen as a kind of residual category, a rapidly fading anachronism in a world transformed by urban processes.

Given this trend (a trend once thought to be irreversible) it came as somewhat of a shock to discover, as we did in the early 1970's, that the pace of urbanization was not only slowing down, but was reversing itself. For the first time since the early nineteenth century, non-metropolitan areas were experiencing growth, growth attributable not only to a decline in out-migration (what demographers call increased retention), but more importantly to a totally unforeseen pattern of in-migration from urban areas. People have begun to leave cities for small towns, and as they have done so, the gloomy prophesies of the death of small-town America have begun to give way to an optimistic expectation of a rural renaissance.

Before we deal with this new phenomenon and with its implications for the future of the small town, a few points need be made. In the first place, the growth in non-metropolitan America *is* real, and is not simply a reflection of continuing processes of suburbanization. While most of the growth in the decade of the 70's *did* take place in counties adjacent to urban areas (sixty percent according to Beale[4]) and is thus little more than spillover of what are essentially suburbanites who just happen to live in nominally rural areas, even non-adjacent counties are experiencing growth as a result of population in-migration. The point? It is not someone else's blessing or someone else's problem; it is a phenomenon that is occurring throughout non-metropolitan America which will bring its blessings—and its problems—to all of us.

In the second place, these changes seem to be continuing. While some have seen them as merely a temporary reaction to urban unemployment which will revert to the more historically valid pattern of rural-to-urban migration when economic recovery takes place,[5] it is important to note that they have persisted for a full decade. Preliminary 1980 census data underscore this persistence, for in *all* regions of the country save the South, non-metropolitan growth was higher than metropolitan growth, and in many of the cities of the Northeast, there was an actual decline in urban population.[6] The trend, furthermore, is likely to continue, for unlike migration in previous generations where the motivation was almost exclusively economic, this new migration seems somewhat more a reflection of some very basic concerns about quality of life and thus will quite probably not be as readily affected by perturbations in the national economic situation.[7]

Finally, what is taking place is *not* a wholesale abandonment of urban areas and an equalization of population density across the country. In fact, the number of people involved in this migration is not particularly large (in 1975, for example, it involved a net gain to non-metropolitan areas of only some one hundred and nineteen thousand households[8]). We are and will remain an urban society, not only because a very large proportion of those who migrate into non-metropolitan areas are being balanced by a continuing stream of out-migrants but also because the very fact of metropolitan to non-metropolitan migration urbanizes once rural areas.

There are, however, two less-than-fully appreciated implications of this population shift. First, tempted as we might be to measure gains and losses strictly in terms of numbers, such an approach fails to take adequate account of the very real issue of the quality of a population. Such data as we have suggest that while those who are moving from the cities to the countryside are younger, better educated, and higher in status than those who already live in the area, they are often older, less well-educated, and lower in status than those who leave. The result is that while many small towns experience a net gain in population size, they suffer a net loss in population quality, for the best and brightest of their young are leaving and are not necessarily being replaced.[9] Second, the fact that the numbers are, for the most part, small should not lull us into a false sense of security. What is taking place is not something analogous to the barbarian invasion of Western Europe, but rather a generally slow and often almost imperceptible movement as families come in ones and twos, rather than in hordes. And yet the numbers are not particularly important, because in the long run, *who* moves is far more significant than how many move.

The purpose of this paper is to discuss neither why this return to non-metropolitan areas is taking place (we are not entirely sure), nor who is making the move (one can make general statements, but generalizations conceal a tremendous diversity). Both are impor-tant, and both need to be considered, but my purpose here is to speculate about outcome, about what population shifts are going to mean to the future of the small town.

I would like to suggest three scenarios as representing the most probable situations with which many small towns will have to deal in the coming decades. They are not mutually exclusive, nor do they necessarily represent an exhaustive list of all that may take place. They are simply a sense of what is likely. There is, in fact, a fourth scenario which comes to mind with which I am not going to deal: the ideal situation in which an easily managed number of readily assimilable individuals move into small towns and bring with them the kinds of skills which will attract the kinds of jobs that will make the future secure. The reason I do not propose to consider this fourth scenario is simply that such a fortuitous convergence of factors is, for the vast majority of small towns, highly unlikely, and to dwell upon it is to engage in sheer utopianism.

Scenario I: Things as Usual

As dramatic and as unexpected as the reversal of non-metropolitan population growth has been, it must be realized that not all small towns are growing. One-third of all non-metropolitan communities had relatively stable populations during the decade of the '70's, and another one-fifth continued to experience significant population decline. Some of these communities are in the Northeast, where agricultural towns and retail-service centers have continued a withering away that for many of them began before the Revolution. Stable or declining, too, are many of the communities in the Great Plains and the Corn Belt (except for a few isolated areas in Kansas, Iowa, and Indiana), as well as those in the tobacco- and cotton-growing regions from North Carolina to the Mississippi Delta. What these latter groups have in common is a reliance upon relatively undiversified commercial agriculture and a lack of proximity to both major urban areas and sophisticated transportation arteries.

What is the plight of the communities in these areas? In spite of what one might expect, the impact of continued population decline is not necessarily bad, for in many areas, particularly in the Great Plains, out-migration has been beneficial, for as it has apparently increased the value of the remaining work force, it has led to what Hansen calls "the greatest acceleration of non-metropolitan income in the country."[10] But this prosperity seems to be the exception, for in many towns in other areas, stability means stagnation and decline means disaster, for there is a clear picture of economic dislocation. These towns face diminishing employment opportunities (a particularly severe problem in the areas within which agribusiness is still in its ascendancy), a deteriorating housing stock, and chronic fiscal crises as population falls and as the tax base erodes. What is particularly ominous is that in many of these areas there are still too many people relative to labor demand, and as the technological revolution in agriculture continues, the replacement of people by machines will continue as well and lead to still more unemployment and still more out-migration.

How can a town stay in or join the ranks of the unchanging? It really is not very difficult. Offer as few services as possible (this has the added advantage of keeping taxes low) and do as little as possible to attract attention to the community. That is how one can keep from growing, and that is also an excellent way to run the risk of committing a sort of socio-economic suicide.

A more serious problem is that a great many small towns are going to have great difficulty growing even if they want to. A 1981 study sponsored by the Council of State Planning Agencies concluded that one-half to two-thirds of the nation's communities could not support modern development without huge capital investments in facilities.[11]

A small town does not have to grow, and residents of many small towns quite correctly fear that growth will endanger their way of life, but they are going to have to retain at least the population they have, for if they do not they are going to die person by person. The small town that does not change is not going to be able to hold onto its young, and as the young go, the town's existence goes with them. Can a town refuse to grow and try to remain forever the same? It is not really impossible, but it is both highly unlikely and extremely dangerous, for to try to do so is to flirt with decline, decay, and with eventual disappearance.

Scenario II: Suburban Spillover

As I have already pointed out, the majority of non-metropolitan growth in the decade of the '70's took place in counties adjacent to metropolitan areas and was not so much a return to the countryside (although that motive has clearly played a part) as it was a case of suburban spillover. This is clearly the pattern throughout most of the country and is particularly acute in Sunbelt states. According to preliminary 1980 Census data, of the nineteen metropolitan areas which had population increases of ten percent or more during the decade, thirteen were in the Sunbelt (including California) with Phoenix (fifty-five percent increase) and Fort Lauderdale-Hollywood, Florida, (sixty-two percent increase) leading the list, and of these, the growth of five involved the co-optation of adjacent, previously non-metropolitan counties.[12]

Clearly in these counties population is growing, and as it grows, the tax base grows with it, restoring to many once declining communities the prospect of prosperity. Yet I would suggest that such growth is not without its consequences, the majority of which are the result of the population increase itself. These I will deal with in a few moments. What I would like to focus upon *here* are the kinds of consequences, positive as well as negative, that are unique to the phenomena of suburban spillover.

In general, the potential for rapid growth in communities adjacent to metropolitan areas is quite high, particularly where suburban outer rings are already densely built over. As a result when a community is "discovered," it is likely to grow very quickly as "first families" serve as a magnet to others. Initially there is a simple increase in population, but after a lag of as much as several years, services begin to follow to take advantage of new population concentrations.

One of the first things to change is the retail structure of the community, a gain to the degree to which goods and services were previously unavailable, but a loss to the degree to which new businesses compete with and, in many instances, displace local retail merchants who are either unwilling to change, or who are so undercapitalized that change is impossible.

If the magnet for in-migrants is affordable housing (and housing in non-metropolitan areas is often remarkably inexpensive by urban standards), the result will be a housing boom and a rise in housing prices which, although it can have a very healthy impact on property-tax assessments, can also price housing out of the hands of the indigenous population. This housing problem is particularly important when the attraction is not housing *per se,* but rather the availability of a stock of affordable and restorable historically and/or architectually significant homes. To certain kinds of in-migrants, particularly young professionals, a unique small-town resource is the kind of housing which offers amenities no longer affordable in cities and not available at any price in suburbia: quality construction with quality materials, huge yards with fine old

trees, high ceilings, wide porches, and, most elusively, "charm."
The problem lies in the fact that housing of this sort is in very short
supply and, as a result, is subject to rapid inflation due to inexor-
able market pressures.

Conflicts in values and in lifestyles are inevitable, for while newcomers to a community often see themselves as saviours coming to
deliver the town and its homes from oblivion, they are often seen
by long-time residents as a threat to a long-established way of life.
Rather than fitting in, they often try to make over the community
conform to their sense of "the way it's supposed to be," a way that
is, as often as not, tied to a nineteenth-century vision of small-town
life. Land-use conflicts can also occur as the proliferation of newcomers attracts purveyors of goods and services of limited relevance to the lifestyles and needs of long-time residents: fashionable
boutiques (all patterned after "quaint" country stores) selling the
avant rather than the practical, trendy little specialty shops, and
precious little restaurants complete with checkered tablecloths and
hurricane lamps. The result? Resentments, as long-time residents
see their towns become playgrounds for the affluent.

Another potential problem is that of a baby boomlet. Certainly
the reproductive patterns of newcomers will never equal those of
the baby-boom years of the late 1940's and 1950's—values have
changed far too much for that to occur—but since those who are in
the vanguard of the in-migrants are young, there is likely to be
considerable impact, particularly in communities where birth rates
have been down for decades.[13] While nothing is likely to happen
immediately save the development of a rather lucrative practice for
the town's obstetrician, in time infants grow into school-age children who need to be educated. The problem is not only one of
having to build schools (itself enough of a problem) but also one
that endures after the boomlet passes, for many communities, having built school after school to accommodate a surge of children,
will, after a decade or so, have to close school after school as the
surge passes, leaving in its wake a huge burden of bonded indebt-
edness.

Let me make it clear that in spite of what may seem a wholly
pessimistic view of the situation, the small town faced with suburban spillover is not entirely the loser, and from some points of view

has as much to gain as to lose. More stores mean more jobs, and for many small towns, jobs and a diversification of employment opportunities are of vital importance. More building—or in the case of an historic/architectural preservation motive for in-migration, more remodeling—means a viable building-trades industry and the potential for the development of locally based services. More people mean more taxes, taxes which may well offset inevitable in-migrant demands for improved and expanded public-sector services. The point I wish to make is a very basic one: we often put ourselves in a terribly disadvantageous position by asking the right questions in the wrong fashion. We try to carry out a sort of cost-benefit analysis, but all too often do it backwards. We tend to ask, What is it going to cost them and how are we going to benefit?", rather than asking, "What benefits are they going to expect, and what is it going to cost us?" It makes quite a difference how you ask the question, for if asked in the wrong way, the question gets answers that are often, I believe, far too optimistic.

Scenario III: Economic Renaissance
Of all the possibilities for the future of the small town the most intriguing, and yet the most uncertain in terms of outcome, is economic renaissance. Although only a small proportion of small towns not adjacent to metropolitan areas have, as yet, undergone significant growth, the potential is clearly there, and the decade of the '80's may well prove that the age of small-town America is once again upon us. It is in this realm that the questions of who the in-migrants are and why they are moving takes on particular significance, for the composition and motivation of the in-migrant stream has tremendous importance for any discussion of outcome.

While generalization is always fraught with the danger of over-simplication, and while much of our knowledge is based upon highly particularistic studies, there are at least four distinct groups involved in the migration, each of which has a relatively distinct motivation.

The first group, which is in some regions of the country the largest, is made up of returnees: individuals who, having left non-metropolitan America as part of the post-World War II flight from the countryside, are beginning to return, leaving behind them a situation of chronic urban unemployment and seeking to resume a way of life which, once left, came to be appreciated. Such data as we have pertaining to this group clearly suggest that social as distinct from economic factors are paramount in their decisions to return.[14] The size of this migration component is highly variable from location to location. In the Ozarks, for example, a survey found that forty-three percent of the in-migrants were returnees,[15] a pattern probably being repeated in Appalachia as well as in parts of the Delta South where the return of blacks is (or, at least, is likely to become) an important component in growth. Nationally, Long and DeAre report that 6.8% of the respondents in the 1975 Annual Housing Survey moved from metropolitan to non-metropolitan areas to be closer to relatives,[16] a figure which probably significantly underestimates the size of the returnee component, as many are returning not to kin but to a way of life.

The second group is made up of retirees whose exodus from urban America has been made possible by a relatively high standard of living underwritten by pensions and by Social Security. This group makes up a large portion of the Sunbelt migration stream, although they are to be found moving to other areas as well: Price and Clay report on one town in Michigan, for example, where over forty-five percent of the migrant stream was made up of individuals sixty-five or older.[17] Why do they migrate? Part of the motivation is clearly related to a desire for a change in quality of life which has become paramount as they are freed from the locational demands of regular employment. Important too are economic factors, for most seek to make their usually fixed incomes go further in areas with lower costs of living. Nationally this group is quite small (Long and DeAre report 5.6% on the basis of the 1975 Annual Housing Survey[18]), but numbers are deceptive, for these people not only are highly fiscally conservative but can often wield political power far in excess of what their numbers would suggest because a very high proportion of them vote. As the editor of a small-town newspaper in California complained: "They'll come out of the desert in wheelchairs and walkers to vote down anything."[19]

The third group might be termed the workers, individuals for whom migration is the result of the combined effects of urban unemployment and of the decentralization and relocation of economic units from urban to rural areas.[20] Since the 1960's there has been a massive exodus of labor-intensive manufacturing out of cities into rural areas, particularly those in the South. Motivated by technological improvements in transportation and communication (which makes proximity between productive units unnecessary) and drawn by an availability of relatively inexpensive land, generally lower levels of taxation, and the existence of a huge pool of underemployed, low-cost, non-unionized, and efficient workers, industry has come and has brought with it badly needed jobs, jobs which, in turn, attract workers. Of particular, although at the moment highly localized importance, is the economic boom brought about by the post-1973 search for domestic supplies of energy. The impact of this kind of growth on small communities can be devastating because of the speed with which it can occur.

The fourth, and probably the most important group both in numbers and potential impact, might best be termed the disenchanted. For a great many young, highly educated, middle- and upper-middle-class professionals, there has occurred over the last decade a progressive disenchantment with city living and an emerging fascination with the kind of life the small town can offer. For this group the advantages of living in the city have declined as retail trade and job opportunities have begun to move out of urban areas. Crime, deteriorating environment, taxes, and the feelings of anonymity and impersonality that urban areas seem to engender had led, as well, to a change in attitude toward the city. The city has, for many, become a symbol of society gone wrong, of poverty and decay, of crime and corruption. Non-metropolitan areas, in contrast, offer all that a city lacks: a simple, safe lifestyle; a personal world where one can establish personal and rewarding relationships; and an environment with none of the noise or congestion or filth characteristic of our largest cities. Economic factors too play a part, for small towns in the '70's and '80's offer both occupational opportunities and at least the possibility of alternative careers not readily pursuable in cities: the opportunity to go into business for oneself (often by buying local businesses), or to pursue as a livelihood what in a city would be only an avocation.[21]

What are the consequences of this economic renaissance in non-metropolitan America likely to be? Sometimes the changes that take place—changes that are inevitable—will occur painlessly and will bring to small towns not only needed tax dollars but a new vitality as well. In addition, newcomers often bring with them desperately needed skills which can substantially improve the quality of life for the town and for its people. Many small towns are finding, for example, that they no longer have difficulty attracting physicians and dentists, lawyers and teachers as permanent residents. In other places, however, the changes can be very painful, for when the numbers that migrate are too large to permit easy assimilation, and when the newcomers are different in social characteristics and values from the long-term residents, difficulties are inevitable.

Regardless of the specific makeup of the in-migrant stream, there is going to be an increase in demand for services as newcomers overload the carrying capacity of both the local job market and local service systems. Common to all newcomers is going to be a demand for urban-style services that are not always available in non-metropolitan areas. One very common and extremely expensive demand is for community wastewater treatment and community water systems, demands made particularly burdensome by inceasingly stringent state and Federal regulations.[22]

Special populations will, furthermore, demand special services. If a large component of the in-migrant stream is made up of retirees, services and facilities specific to their needs (primarily health care but also law enforcement and a variety of social services) are going to be in particular demand. If, on the other hand, the stream has a large component of young adults, education can very rapidly become a pressing issue.

The worker and returnee components represent a source of potential difficulty as well, for in spite of some fundamental differences in motivation, both have the same immediate goal: employment. To the degree to which jobs are the magnet (and this will be increasingly the case *if* decentralization tendencies continue), their migration has the capability of overwhelming the available stock of jobs, and as they are often better educated and more highly skilled than the long-term residents, they are generally able to compete successfully for what jobs *are* available. The result will be an expansion of the ranks of the unemployed. In a very real sense, their migration may simply have the effect of moving unemployment problems from the cities to the small towns.

As demands for services and facilities increase, many small towns are going to be faced with severe financial difficulties because of the extremely high cost of necessary capital improvements. While the most readily appreciated crises are economic, there are other consequences as well, for the resentment of long-term residents when they are called upon to pay the same share as the newcomers foreshadows a potential breakdown in community solidarity. This problem can reach almost catastrophic proportions when the source of growth is energy exploitation, as it is in the Southwest and throughout Appalachia, for not only do the in-migrants have little long-term interest in the community (most are highly transient construction workers or "gypsy" miners) but their sheer numbers necessitate the development of service systems and facilities which will eventually stand empty as the boom passes, leaving empty mobile homes and empty community treasuries.

Separate from, but intimately connected with, the problem of providing services and facilities are problems which stem from the diversity of values and expectations which characterize the different groups in the community. In the long run, these "culture clashes" are probably less easily resolved and more detrimental to community well-being than any of the more immediate fiscal difficulties. There is virtually no aspect of community life that can escape the problem, for conflicts can emerge not only between newcomers and long-time residents but also between different groups of newcomers. Education, in particular, often becomes a battleground between those for whom expansion and upgrading of educational facilities is of paramount importance, and those for whom the expanding and upgrading promise only higher taxes. In many communities, retirees in particular have successfully blocked bond issue after bond issue in a revolt against rising educational costs. Often at issue as well is educational philosophy, as disputes emerge between those who favor traditional book-centered education and those who favor non-traditional life-centered education.

One of the most important, and certainly one of the most unexpected conflicts to emerge, has to do with the fact of growth itself: not only how to grow but often whether or not to continue to grow. Study after study has found that newcomers are often outspoken in their demand that future growth of the community be halted: Graber probably came closest to touching the heart of the issue when she quoted one of the residents of the town that was the subject of her study as saying, " '[E]veryone wants to be the last person to move' " in, and then " 'they want to close the gate.' "[23]

The causes of this "last-man-in" mentality are two-fold: in the first place, many (primarily the so-called "disenchanted") bring with them a vision of small-town life which is simply not real, for the small towns to which they have moved do not really exist and probably never have. Many of them are living out a fantasy within which they try to make time itself stand still. Less extreme, and probably far more common, is the very real fear that growth will forever change the way of life that first brought them to non-metropolitan small towns; little good is assumed to be possible from continued growth and development. What is important about this motive is that it often underlies community disputes that rage on in other terms. Suddenly the sort of economic development which can be a panacea to the town's economic woes seems to trigger conflicts between competing interests. A town manages to attract light industry, and what happens? Does everyone rejoice? Sometimes, but more often of late, conflict is the result: the re-tirees start worrying aloud about industrial pollution; the intellec-tuals threaten town fathers with everything from the Sierra Club to Barry Commoner for proposing to build a factory *there*, and every-one becomes suddenly preoccupied with longer and more detailed environmental impact statements. The problem is not usually one of pollution, or a piece of ground, or a piece of paper, although these may come to take on a tremendous symbolic importance. The problem is one of resistance to further growth, and this is one of the most difficult problems with which small towns are going to have to deal.

Conclusion

What then are small towns to do? I am certainly not proposing that communities across non-metropolitan America seek to erect huge walls to keep everyone out. In the first place, walls are very expensive and very hard to maintain, and in the second place, the inmigrants *do* have something to offer. They bring dollars to revitalize depleted treasuries and to revive long moribund economies, and they bring a kind of vitality. They bring as well skepticism, for by rejecting the idea that things must remain as they have always been, they bring change—change that is often painful, but change which is in the long run to the advantage of all.

It is not simply an issue of growing and changing versus not growing and remaining forever the same. That is a false and misleading dichotomy. In large part, it *is* "damned if you do, and damned if you don't," but I believe that a community can avoid the worst consequences of the situation by eschewing the easy solutions that are often thrust upon it, for the answer does *not* lie in a paranoid avoidance of growth any more than in the wholehearted acceptance of growth at any price. The price that we pay for each of these is, I believe, too high to be endured. Change is inevitable, and the real question is not change versus no change, but what kinds of changes will be accepted with what kinds of consequences. Small towns cannot halt change—or at least I do not believe that they should make an effort to—but they can minimize its impact and use change to their advantage.

There are two suggestions that I might make—obvious ones, but the obvious are often the most elusive. First, growth management. Small towns probably can neither stop growth once it has begun nor start growth if the circumstances are not right, but they *can* control it. As I have pointed out already, what is important *in the long run* is not numbers but rather the social and cultural characteristics of those who migrate, and this can to a degree be controlled. Small towns can actively seek to attract the kind of people who best fit their image of their future. This brings us quite directly to my second suggestion: pre-emptive planning. Small towns cannot preclude change, but they can affect its direction. It is terribly dangerous to improvise a growth policy, and yet that is what a large number of small communities are doing. The small town must know early on what it is and where it wishes to go, and must keep that knowledge clearly before it as it meets the future.

NOTES

[1] Commission on Population Growth and the American Future, *Population and the American Future* (New York: Signet Books, 1972); Claude S. Fischer, "Urban Malaise," *Social Forces*, 52 (December 1973), 221–235.

[2] Lewis Mumford, *The Culture of Cities* (New York: Harcourt, Brace and Co., 1938).

[3] Everett S. Lee, Jane M. Wilkie, and Leon F. Bouvier, "The Desertion of Our Countryside," *Population Profiles*, No. 7 (1973).

[4] Calvin L. Beale, "Renewed Growth in Rural Communities," *The Futurist* (August 1975), 196–202.

[5] John F. Kain, "Implications of Declining Metropolitan Populations on Housing Markets," in *Post-Industrial America: Metropolitan Decline and Inter-Regional Job Shifts*, eds. George Sternlieb and James W. Hughes (New Brunswick: The Center for Urban Policy Research, 1975), 221–227.

[6] The situation in the South is not a deviation from an otherwise nation-wide pattern but represents one of the paradoxes of non-metropolitan growth, for as non-metropolitan counties grow in population, they become urban.

[7] Gordon F. DeJong and Craig Humphrey, "Selected Characteristics of Metropolitan-to-Nonmetropolitan Area Migrants: A Study of Population Redistribution in Pennsylvania," *Rural Sociology*, 41 (Winter 1976) 526–538; Louis A. Ploch, "The Reversal in Migration Patterns: Some Rural Development Consequences," *Rural Sociology*, 45 (Summer 1978), 293–303; James D. Williams and Andrew J. Sofranko, "Motivations for the Inmigration Component of Population Turnabout in Nonmetropolitan Areas," *Demography*, 16 (May 1979), 239–255.

[8] Larry H. Long and Diana DeAre, *Migration to Nonmetropolitan Areas: Appraising the Trend and Reasons for Moving*, Special Demographic Analysis, CDS-80-2 (Washington, D.C.: U.S. Government Printing Office, 1980).

[9] William Alonso, "Metropolis Without Growth," *Public Interest*, 53 (Fall 1978), 68–86; Daniel T. Lichtor, Tim B. Heaton, and Glenn V. Fuguitt, "Trends in the Selectivity of Migration Between Metropolitan and Nonmetropolitan Areas: 1955–1975," *Rural Sociology*, 44 (Winter 1979), 645–666.

[10] Niles M. Hansen, *The Future of Nonmetropolitan America: Studies in the Reversal of Rural and Small Town Population Decline* (Lexington, Mass.: D. C. Heath and Co., 1973), 17.

[11] John Herbers, "Nationwide Renewal of Public Works Urged," *New York Times*, 5 April 1981.

[12] John Herbers, "Many Urban Areas Gained Population as Cities Declined," *New York Times*, 1 February 1981.

[13] For a discussion of rural birth rates, see Lee, Wilkie, and Bouvier, "The Desertion of Our Countryside."

[14] See, for example, Rex R. Campbell and D. M. Johnson, "Propositions on Counter-Stream Migration," *Rural Sociology*, 41 (Spring 1976), 127–145.

[15] Williams and Sofranko, "Motivation for the Inmigrant Component of Population Turnabout."

[16] Long and DeAre, "Migration to Nonmetropolitan Areas."

[17] Michael L. Price and Daniel C. Clay, "Structural Disturbances in Rural Communities: Some Repercussions of the Migration Turnabout in Michigan," *Rural Sociology*, 45 (Winter 1980), 591–607.

[18] Long and DeAre, "Migration to Nonmetropolitan Areas."

[19] Quoted in William E. Blundell, "New Rural Migration Overburdens and Alters Once-Sleepy Hamlets," *The Wall Street Journal*, 3 July 1980.

[20] Alan Kirschenbaum, "Patterns of Migration from Metropolitan to Nonmetropolitan Areas: Changing Ecological Factors Affecting Family Mobility," *Rural Sociology*, 36 (September 1971), 315–325; Larry H. Long, "Back to the Countryside and Back to the City in the Same Decade," in *Back to the City: Issues in Neighborhood Renovation*, ed. Shirley B.

Laska and Daphne Spain (New York: Permagon Press, 1980), 61–76.

[21] DeJong and Humphrey, "Selected Characteristics of Metropolitan-to-Nonmetropolitan Area Migrants"; Ploch, "The Reversal in Migration Patterns."

[22] Department of Housing and Urban Development, *Second Biennial Report on National Urban Policy* (Washington, D.C.: U.S. Government Printing Office, 1980).

[23] Edith E. Graber, "Newcomers and Oldtimers: Growth and Change in a Mountain Town," *Rural Sociology*, 39 (Winter 1974), 510.

The Small Town:
Magnet and Storehouse

RICHARD ADICKS

One of the many places where history and literature meet is on the main street of the American small town. On the one hand, the small town has been—and still is—a kind of magnet, attracting people who expect to find there something they seek—friends, money, perhaps just the chance to be left alone. On the other, the small town has provided a storehouse of memories for writers brought up in small towns. As a magnet, the small town has historical value. As a storehouse, it has literary value. Yet these values are not far apart. Just as the novelist or the poet has invented character or incident out of the storehouse of memory provided for him by the small town, so has the occasional entrepreneur or benefactor, sometimes used a small town as a means for creating and furthering a cherished conception of himself.

From the beginning people, including, of course, writer and entrepreneur, have reacted to one of the four phases through which the American small town has passed—as frontier settlement, as established institution, as target for attack and satire, and as an institution struggling to hold its place in a rapidly changing society.

As long as there was a frontier, the town was measured against it, and a person loved it or loathed it according to what he thought of the frontier, the wilderness. The early Puritans feared the forest and thus sought the town, which they vainly hoped could be established as a Biblical community. Though Washington Irving loved the small towns that he wrote about, simply because he enjoyed human society, many other Romantics disparaged the town and sought the forest as a sanctuary of virtue. Fenimore Cooper's Leatherstocking fled the towns, and Henry David Thoreau removed himself to the fringe of Concord.

As soon as the wilderness was overcome, the small town became its own measure, acquiring a reputation for simplicity, honesty, neighborliness, and clean living. When Mark Twain published *The Adventures of Tom Sawyer* in 1876 he drew on all of the storehouse of nostalgia that Hannibal, Missouri, afforded him. This same perception of the small town, continuing well into the twentieth century, pervades Thornton Wilder's *Our Town* (1936). In that play Grover's Corners embodies a nostalgic ideal of honesty, kindness, love, good humor—with little to balance against them. (Even Tom Sawyer's home town had the sinister Injun Joe in it.)

If the second stage in the perception of small towns breathed the air of sentimentality, it was also a time when small towns could offer rewards in money or popular recognition. Often small towns have been dominated or exploited by men who made their homes in those same towns, but one man, Henry Foster, born in a small town in Vermont, set himself up as the patron of one small town in New York and another in Florida. For Henry Foster, as much as for any novelist, the small town was raw material that he could shape as he wished, and in doing so he could put himself forward as the sort of man he wanted to be seen as being. The difference between Foster and the novelist is that whereas the novelist uses the power of words and imagination to create a fictitious character, Henry Foster used the power of money and prestige—with, to his credit, a considerable bit of generous good will thrown in—to create an idealized picture of Henry Foster as a philanthropist.

The sixth of seven children, Henry Foster was born in 1821 in Norwich, Vermont.[1] After his father's linseed oil factory failed, the family moved to a farm near Rochester, New York, in 1835. In the subsequent years Henry and his brothers and sisters learned not only thrift, but also the lessons of faith and devoutness. Henry himself showed an evangelical bent early in life, at the age of ten telling his sister, who had chided him for attending too many revival meetings, "Martha, do you think I have so much religion that I do not need more? The best way to get it is by helping others."

On that idea, Henry Foster built a reputation for philanthropy. Having received his M.D. degree in 1848 from a medical school that is now part of a Western Reserve University, he went to work as medical director of a spa in New York, where he learned the techniques of hydrotherapy, at that time a fad throughout Europe and America that had encouraged the establishment of spas for treatment of various illnesses.

When Dr. Foster moved to Clifton Springs, New York, in 1850 and gained enough financial support to found a new sanitarium there, Clifton Springs had already been known for years as a spa, originally under the name of Sulphur Springs. Foster made his sanitarium so successful that he was able to become sole owner by 1867. In 1860 he was listed in the U.S. Census as owning only $20,000 in real estate; by 1870 he claimed $200,000 worth. When the sanitarium prospered, he used the profits to provide free care for ministers and their families and for teachers.

By 1864, exhausted from overwork, Dr. Foster began to leave the sanitarium for two months every winter and spend those two months in some other place. After the Civil War, he started travelling in Florida. But he was a man who liked to achieve things, and mere hunting was not enough. Looking for a place to build a winter home, he chose the Lake Jesup community, later to be called Oviedo, near the upper St. Johns River. There his presence had a stabilizing effect. According to his biographer, religious meetings started in all seriousness, men hung up their hunting guns on Sunday, and a rowdy element in the community adopted the doctor's disciplined ways. And they became his friends.

His philanthropic activities in the community began when he took Mrs. Mattie Gwynn, a woman so ill that he was convinced she could not live much longer if she remained where she was, to his sanitarium in Clifton Springs. There she stayed for nearly a year and the following winter came home cured. Moreover, the spiritual climate at the sanitarium had had such an effect on her that she became an evangelist in the community. Foster's biographer says, "A great revival followed, and continued until every adult save seven, within a radius of six miles was converted."

In 1874 Foster bought twenty-six acres on the north shore of Lake Charm from Walter Gwynn, Mattie's husband, and there built his winter home. He was also buying other land, especially groves. In the early 1870's he set out, at nearby Gee Hammock, a grove that became his pride, along with a smaller grove near Lake Charm. By the middle '80's he could claim nearly fifty acres of groves, together with uncultivated land, for an aggregate worth of $100,000. One guidebook on Florida mentioned the Gee Hammock grove as one of the most beautiful in the state. In 1889 he reckoned that it had paid for itself, including eight per cent interest on his investment, and that year he turned down $50,000 for it. Six years later, after the freeze of 1895, the grove was worthless.

Henry Foster stood over the young community like a generous father, putting a stop to the extortion of loan sharks and finding favorable interest rates for the settlers. He employed both blacks and whites, and he gave generously to the establishment of churches, and possibly to schools as well. His contributions to the fledgling Methodist church are documented in the church records. When the parishioners built their new church with their own labor in 1878, Dr. and Mrs. Foster furnished it, sending to New York for a pulpit, an altar rail, pews, and Estey reed organ, and stained-glass windows, some of which furnishings are still in the church. Grateful, the little congregation named their church Foster Chapel, and Foster Chapel it remained for eighty years. Each year he gave the chapel $50, and in the bumper year of 1890 he gave $100. He probably also gave money to the two Baptist churches, one for whites and one for blacks, that were established in the 1870's.

Among the permanent effects of Dr. Foster's activity in the community was his development of Lake Charm as a resort and winter home for Northern visitors. Soon he persuaded a number of well-to-do friends and patients to move to Florida and build homes on Lake Charm, and in 1888 he encouraged his neighbors to form the Lake Charm Improvement Company to improve the property around the lake. In 1882 he built the Lake Charm Memorial Chapel as a memorial to his brother William, and soon thereafter a parsonage next door, which served as a kind of winter hotel for visiting missionaries and ministers from the North who would bring their families and come with Dr. Foster to Florida. During the winter, the Memorial Chapel would echo to the sermons of such noted preachers of the day as John R. Mott, Samuel Hawley Adams, and Methodist Bishop William X. Ninde.

Foster sought also to provide solutions to the problem of transportation costs facing him and other citrus growers—first with the establishment in 1882 of the Lake Jesup Steamboat Company and later in 1889, with the founding of the Oviedo, Lake Charm, and Lake Jesup Railroad. The steamboat company came to an early end when the steamboat *Isis*, in which the company owned an eleven-fifteenths interest, sank. The railroad company, however, did have some success in forcing down shipping costs; for $25.00 the company purchased a pole car on which oranges could be poled to the nearest wharf, about a mile from town, to be shipped by steamboat.

The Lake Jesup Steamboat Company, the Lake Charm Improvement Company, the Oviedo, Lake Charm and Lake Jesup Railroad—none of these lasted. Each was formed to meet an immediate need, and no more. Not only did new circumstances call for meeting needs in other ways, but also the participants started dragging their feet, pleading lack of money, looking for the wealthy doctor to put up more money. In some letters from stockholders there appears a veiled resentment, as if to say, "Sure, that's all right for a rich man like Dr. Foster, but what about me?" Dr. Foster's philanthropy supplied the material things that he set out to supply, but sometimes it may have had the bad effect of seducing people into the easy habit of waiting for largesse to flow.

After the devastating freeze in February 1895, Dr. Foster's friends from the North were too discouraged at the loss of their groves ever to come back, and the well-to-do Lake Charm community broke up. The Fosters, however, returned year after year, and, with that persistence that had always been characteristic of him, Foster pruned the deadwood from his trees and nourished them into life again. But it takes many years to bring ruined trees back into production, and Dr. Foster did not have that many years left. Six winters later, too sick to make the annual trip to Florida, he died.

Though his name has been virtually forgotten in Oviedo, Foster's imposing old sanitarium, now a retirement home, still stands as a memorial to the public-spirited physician in Clifton Springs. In two small towns, Henry Foster had found what he was looking for: the chance to leave his mark, to serve as a community benefactor and patron.

In the attacks on the small town that characterized the third stage of reaction to the small town, writers were prominent. One of the most noteworthy attacks on small-town hypocrisy was Mark Twain's "The Man That Corrupted Hadleyburg" (1899). The people of Hadleyburg are so complacent, so proud of their reputation for honesty, that they have chosen "Lead Us Not Into Temptation" as their town motto. A stranger, disgusted at their smugness, shows them up when he pretends to leave gold to be given to someone who has done him a kindness, then secretly lets all the town's leading citizens know what the words are that will identify the proper recipient of the gold. He sits back and enjoys the mad scramble as the pillars of the community all try to claim the sack, which proves to contain only lead. In the end, the town changes its motto to "Lead Us Into Temptation," to show that they have learned that true virtue must be tested.

The early years of the twentieth century saw a good deal of literature that measured small towns not against the simple virtues of the wilderness, as Fenimore Cooper had done, but against an abstract standard of freedom and of self-realization. Again and again the small town was found wanting. Sinclair Lewis's small towns in *Main Street* (1920) and *Babbitt* (1922) were vainly given to a hollow boosterism. Edwin Arlington Robinson patterned his fictional Tilbury Town after Gardiner, Maine, and gave it a voice in his first volume of poems in 1896. Robinson, responding to a critic's charge that he saw the world as a prison house, replied, "The world is not a prison house, but a kind of spiritual kindergarten where bewildered infants are trying to spell God with the wrong blocks." The small town became for him a window through which that kindergarten might be viewed. Edgar Lee Masters' *Spoon River Anthology* (1915) and Sherwood Anderson's *Winesburg, Ohio* (1919) gave equally poignant expression to a feeling that the small town had betrayed the promise that had attracted Henry Foster and others of his generation.

Writers have also been prominent in treating the small town in its fourth stage of development—its struggle to hold a place in a rapidly changing society. In the 1930's the literature of small-town life began to exhibit certain regular conventions, four of which are the use of names, the establishment of a center for activity and observation, the characterization of the wise older guide, and the theme of escape.

The most obvious of the conventions is the use of names. In small-town fiction, everybody who belongs has a name, which is to say that everybody has an identity. In Faulkner's *The Hamlet* (1931–40), for example, much of the action is affected by the horse trader known only as "the Texan," but he does not have a name because he is an outsider. Everybody else is named, with the most colorful names reserved for the Snopeses, as numerous as boll weevils: names like Flem Snopes, I. O. Snopes, Wallstreet Panic Snopes, and so on.

Important to the setting of small-town literature is usually a place where people of the town loiter in order to comment on the action of the story and sometimes to create the flavor of the town. The importance of such a place is emphasized by the novelist/anthropologist, Zora Neale Hurston in her autobiography, *Dust Tracks on a Road* (1942), where she says of her home town, Eatonville, an all-black town in central Florida:

> There were the two churches, Methodist and Baptist, and the school. Most people would say that such institutions are always the great influences in any town. They would say that because it sounds like the thing that ought to be said. But I know that Joe Clarke's store was the heart and spring of the town. Men sat around the store on boxes and benches and passed this world and the next one through their mouths. The right and wrong, the who, when and why was passed on, and nobody doubted the conclusions. Women stood around there on Saturday nights and had it proved to the community that their husbands were good providers, put all of their money in their wives' hands and generally glorified them. . . . There were no discreet nuances of life on Joe Clarke's porch. There was open kindnesses, anger, hate, love, envy and its kinfolks, but all emotions were naked, and nakedly arrived at. It was a case of "make it and take it." You got what your strengths would bring you. This was not just true of Eatonville. This was the spirit of that whole new part of the state at the time, as it always is where men settle new lands.[2]

In fiction, Varner's store in Faulkner's *The Hamlet*, where the hangers-on take perverse delight in watching Flem Snopes bamboozle his neighbors, the "Old Kentucky Home" boarding house in Thomas Wolfe's *Look Homeward Angel* (1929), where varied personalities emerge and merge, the pool hall and the humdrum "picture show" house in Larry McMurtry's *The Last Picture Show* (1966)—these serve to focus town life, to assert the claims of the community.

Because many novels of small-town life are novels about growing up, an important presence is often that of an older, wiser guide.

Young Ike McCaslin in Faulkner's *The Bear* (1935–42) learns to hunt from the old woodsman, Sam Fathers. Eugene Gant in Thomas Wolfe's *Look Homeward, Angel* looks up to his discontented older brother, Ben. Sonny and Duane in Larry McMurtry's *The Last Picture Show*, estranged from their own parents, find a surrogate father in an old man called Sam the Lion. Significantly, Faulkner's Sam Fathers, Wolfe's Ben Gant, and McMurtry's Sam the Lion die at some crucial turning point in the story, paving the way for the main character's passage to a new stage in his life.

Finally, one distinctive feature of most small-town fiction is the theme of getting out, of escaping from the town. Tom Sawyer never wanted to get away from his town. In fact, at the end of *The Adventures of Tom Sawyer* he talks Huck Finn into staying, using the provocative argument that if he will stay and be outwardly respectable, he can become a notorious robber along with Tom and the other boys. However, by the time he gets to the end of *Adventures of Huckleberry Finn* (1884), Huck, having decided that town life is not for him, declares that he will "light out for the territory." Sherwood Anderson gives us a last glimpse of George Willard, the protagonist of *Winesburg, Ohio*, as George is on a train leaving the town that for so long has stifled his dreams. Perhaps Wolfe's Eugene Gant in *Look Homeward, Angel* best expresses the restless yearning to escape: "The first move I ever made, after the cradle, was to crawl from the door, and every move I have made since has been an effort to escape. And now at last I am free from you all, although you may hold me for a few years more. If I am not free, I am at least locked up in my own prison, but I shall get me some beauty, I shall get me some order out of this jungle of my life: I shall find my way out of it yet, though it take me twenty years more—alone."[3]

Three decades later, however, Sonny, the hero of McMurtry's *The Last Picture Show*, has none of the spirit that stirred within Eugene Gant. Sam the Lion tells him that the oil wells around Thalia, Texas, are drying up and that the cattle business is going to peter out; then Sam dies and the picture show screens one last shoot-em-up. But Sonny stays on, his mind barren of the dreams that goaded Huckleberry Finn, George Willard, and Eugene Gant, and settles into a dull routine of meaningless work and tawdry sex. One of the most recent novels about small-town life, however, gives a more hopeful view of the small town. The hero of Robert Penn Warren's *A Place to Come to* (1977) yields when he is young to his mother's insistence that he get away from Dugton, Alabama, but when he is older he nourishes the hope of going back to the little town where he grew up.

The small town has given in a unique way to American culture. Perhaps the reason for its doing so can be seen in a passage from one of Thomas Wolfe's most powerful short stories, "The Lost Boy." In that story, twelve-year-old Grover moves through the public square, thinking of it as "the granite core of changelessness." Of course, we know—and Wolfe knew—that no small town is changeless, but it has managed to wield power in American life and American literature because some people—those drawn to it, those drawn away from it, and those who drew upon it—have entertained the illusion that it was so.

NOTES

[1] The biographical sketch of Henry Foster is adapted from *Oviedo: Biography of a Town*, by Richard Adicks and Donna M. Neely, published and copyrighted by the authors in 1979. Most information about Dr. Foster is from Samuel Hawley Adams, *Life of Henry Foster, M.D.* (Clifton Springs, N.Y., 1912).

[2] Zora Neale Hurston, *Dust Tracks on a Road* (Philadelphia, 1971), pp. 61–62.

[3] Thomas Wolfe, *Look Homeward Angel* (New York, 1929), p. 422.

Chronicles of Change,
Chronicles of Tradition:

Six Books about Mississippi Small Towns
in the 1960s

MICHAEL P. DEAN

A renowned scholar of Southern literature, C. Hugh Holman, provides, by way of omission, an opening to the topic I wish to consider in this essay. He writes:

> Approach it however you will, you will find at the heart of the southern riddle a union of opposites, a condition of instability, a paradox. Calm grace and raw hatred. Polished manners and violence. An intense individualism and intense group pressures toward conformity. A reverence to the point of idolatry of self-determining action and a caste and class structure presupposing an aristocratic hierarchy. A passion for political action and a willingness to surrender to the enslavement of demagogues. A love of the nation intense enough to make the South's fighting men notorious in our wars and the advocacy of interposition and of the public defiance of national law. A region breeding both Thomas Jefferson and John C. Calhoun. If these contradictions are to be brought into focus, if these ambiguities are to be resolved, it must be through the "reconciliation of opposites."[1]

This marshaling of opposites is impressive and, it would seem, considering the wealth of evidence available, accurate. There is, however, one pair of opposites omitted from Holman's list, the very pair that has provided the common theme of the second "Chautauqua in Mississippi," change and tradition.

In the search for "reconciliation of opposites," change and tradition has no part to play in the solution of the "southern riddle." Tradition prevailed, time and again, time out of mind, invariably. The South was *the* land of tradition. (Think of the words of "Dixie"—"old times there are not forgotten"; nor, we might add, were they relinquished. Think of the rallying cry of the demagogues of the 1950s and '60s, "Never. No, Never." Think of the transformation of that phrase by the comedian "Brother" Dave

59

Gardner: "Yesterday, Today, and Forever.") Change was slow, slight, superficial, nearly imperceptible. W. J. Cash's exhaustive *The Mind of the South* proclaims this to us on every page.

And of all the Southern states none was more tradition-bound than Mississippi, and nowhere was tradition more evident than in its small towns. (I might as well say "everywhere," for where was a settlement that could truly claim to be more than a small town?) Mississippi small towns were bastions of tradition; if floods of change swept over other places, these towns remained solid rocks, unchanging, unyielding. But change, indeed, revolution, finally came to them. A flood-tide of change, begun by a single drop in 1954, crested in the early 1960s and swept across them in the remainder of that turbulent decade as surely and as strongly as the 1927 Mississippi River flood rolled across the Delta. I refer, of course, to the civil rights movement and the tradition-shattering changes it produced. James Silver, working with a different metaphor, cites Walt Whitman's 1856 comment on the possibility of slave-holders gaining control in Kansas. Whitman wrote, "Then would the melt begin that would not cool till Kansas should be redeemed, as of course it would be." Silver adds that just such a "melt" began in Mississippi in the early 1960s, a melt that would not cool until change—rapid, disorienting, tradition-challenging— had been assured.[2]

Numerous studies—taking the form of reports, essays, articles, short stories, poems, novels, non-fiction books, television programs, and films, to make only a partial listing—have chronicled the mighty collision of change and tradition in Mississippi during the 1960s. The foci of these studies have been as various as the forms they have taken. One focus, that of the individual caught in the change-tradition confrontation, has proved extremely insightful. The focus of this essay, therefore, will be on the individual viewpoint, seeing it as a productive method of examining the topic of small-town change and tradition as it manifested itself in the small towns of Mississippi during the 1960s. In order to pursue this notion I have selected six books that provide individual viewpoints ranging from that of resident to former resident to non-resident. Three were published in the 1960s; three in the '70s. In order of discussion the books are *Coming of Age in Mississippi* by Anne

Moody, *Letters from Mississippi*, edited by Elizabeth Sutherland, *So the Heffners Left McComb* by Hodding Carter, *Two Faces of Janus: The Saga of Deep South Change* by Oliver Emmerich, *Yazoo: Integration in a Deep-Southern Town* by Willie Morris, and *Witness in Philadelphia* by Florence Mars. These may seem diverse books; my claim of selection may elicit the charge of "random selection." There is, however, a common thread found in all these books; as I have said, they tell of individuals in small towns undergoing the stresses created by the clash of the forces of change and the forces of tradition. And the insights gained by such individuals in such towns in such situations contribute directly to the topic of the second "Chautauqua in Mississippi."

Anne Moody's *Coming of Age in Mississippi* is an autobiography covering the years from 1945 to 1964. It is a first-person narrative of tremendous power, vitality, and insight, yet its tone is one of simplicity and objectivity that reminds the reader of nothing so much as Frederick Douglass's *My Bondage and My Freedom*. However, if Moody were to retitle her book along the lines of Douglass's, she would be forced to omit the latter part of Douglass's phrase. *Coming of Age in Mississippi* has little of freedom in it: it is a chronicle of tradition, tradition that translates into the reality of growing up black in the 1940s and '50s.

Anne Moody spent her childhood in Centreville, a small town in eastern Wilkinson County, nearly astraddle the Wilkinson-Amite county line. She lived briefly in the Wilkinson county seat, Woodville, spent two years in Natchez, two at Tougaloo, interspersed by short interludes in New Orleans. From the summer of 1963 to the book's conclusion in the early summer of 1964, she lived in Canton. The overall image left by the book in the reader's mind is the dual one of Centreville and Canton.

Moody's book serves two purposes for us. First, parts one and two of the book, "Childhood" and "High School" (occupying more than half the text), record the traditional aspects of life in Centreville. We see the rigidity of relationship that governs black and white Centreville. Moody records her awakening to the differences in life-style and expectations prevailing in the two segments of society in her small town. She also records her personal reaction to the differences, a reaction best described, in terms of the situation, as rebellious or resistant. Although the action of the final two sections, "College" and "The Movement," occurs in several locations, we are most impressed by the detailed discussion of her year's work with CORE, primarily in voter registration, in Canton. Here again we see the rigidity of the traditional situation: one town but two worlds, black and white. But here we see not just the agitation for change of an individual, Anne Moody, but also the agitation of several individuals, growing into agitation by so many individuals that Moody's characterization of it as "The Movement" seems the only adequate one.

Coming of Age in Mississippi was published in 1968, but Moody breaks off her narrative, deliberately, I believe, four years earlier, on the eve of the momentous summer of 1964. Foreshadowing that "long hot summer," Anne Moody declares, "I had never witnessed such anticipation in all my life. It seemed that for once in the history of civil rights work in Mississippi something was actually going to be accomplished."[3] But Moody denies, quite rightly, I think, any look at accomplishment or failure. She ends her book with a series of powerful images. As she sits on a bus pulling out of Jackson, bound for Congressional civil rights hearings in Washington, she swiftly catalogs the tradition that her autobiography has borne witness to. She writes:

> I sat there listening to "We Shall Overcome," looking out of the window at the passing Mississippi landscape. Images of all that had happened kept crossing my mind: the Taplin burning, the Birmingham church bombing, Medgar Evers' murder, the blood gushing out of McKinley's head, and all the other murders. I saw the face of Mrs. Chinn as she said, "We ain't big enough to do it by ourselves," C. O.'s face when he gave me that pitiful wave from the chain gang. I could feel the tears welling up in my eyes.
> "Moody . . ." it [sic] was little Gene again interrupting his singing. "Moody, we're gonna git things straight in Washington, huh?"
> I didn't answer him. I knew I didn't have to. He looked as if he knew exactly what I was thinking.
> "I wonder. I wonder."
> We shall overcome, We shall overcome [sic]
> We shall overcome some day.[4]

Her final words, printed in boldface capitals, are "I wonder. I really wonder."[5]

The second of these six books, *Letters from Mississippi*, takes up where Anne Moody's book leaves off. *Letters from Mississippi* delivers what its title promises—hundreds of letters (some fragmentary) from Mississippi, written during the summer of 1964, the "long hot summer" of agitation, "Freedom Summer." Skillful editing and the inclusion of short narrative passages turn the letters into an exciting chronicle, one that often reminds the reader of an adventure story. This sense of adventure is heightened by the immediacy of letters written from the scene of action, as it were, and by the realization of the reality of that scene.

The letters' places of origin—Holly Springs, Ruleville, Carthage, Shaw, Batesville, Moss Point, Mileston, Indianola, Greenwood—form an interlocking grid of Mississippi small towns. And the destinations of the letters—places in the East, the North, the Mid-West, the Far West—remind us that the individual viewpoints expressed are those of non-residents, outsiders—in the terminology of the era, "outside agitators." But these letters reinforce the traditional situation as recorded by Anne Moody. One example from so many will have to suffice:

> There are the old men and women in old clothing whom [sic] you know have little money and none to spare, who stop you as you are leaving the church after addressing the congregation and press a dollar into your hand and say, "I've waited 80 years for you to come and I just have to give you this little bit to let you all know how much we appreciate your coming. I prays for your safety every night. . . ." And then they move down the stone steps and disappear along the red clay road lined with tall green trees and houses tumbling down.[6]

And, like Moody's book, *Letters from Mississippi* leaves us in the midst of the change-tradition clash. However, by carrying us through the summer of 1964, the book allows us a brief glimpse of the beginning of change, the crumbling of tradition. At the end of the book we are told that "the summer project had become the Mississippi Freedom Project" and that even though the "bombings and jailings continued . . . everything seemed different yet the same."[7] In other words, change and tradition were engaged in a monstrous struggle. The final letter in the book, written from the most notorious town of the summer, Philadelphia, carries us out of summer (and out of tradition) and toward fall (and toward change):

As I write this letter I am on the roof of our headquarters observing a sunset I cannot even begin to describe. The hills of red dirt, the pine woods, the mountains and shacks silhouetted against the blood-red sun and clouds, all this and the rest of it takes my breath away. Now and at all such times I find myself possessed by a deep melancholy, a heart-rending feeling for the black and white toilers of this state; both victims of a system that they neither created nor flourish under.

There have been incidents of violence and intimidation but they hardly seem worth noting at a time like this. I only know that I must carry on this struggle that other people have died in, and that some day that system will be changed. . . .[8]

Like *Letters from Mississippi,* Hodding Carter's *So the Heffners Left McComb* chronicles the events of Freedom Summer 1964. Unlike the former's wide-ranging, state-covering approach, however, this book examines with microscopic intensity the fate of one small-town family in that familiar summer. The tale Carter relates is not a pretty one; simply put, he tells of the ostracism and eventual banishment of a prosperous, middle-class white family in Pike County, Mississippi. A home, a business, even a family dog were destroyed because of the willingness of a man and his wife to speak the truth as they saw it. To put it in terms I have employed all along, the Heffners were willing to examine and, consequently, challenge tradition with change. To be more specific, "On the night of July 17, 1964, they served . . . hot tamales to the wrong people, to wit, two young white civil rights workers, one an ordained minister."[9] The Heffners' refusal to disavow their hospitality to the two young men (and, later, to other workers of the 1964 project) brought down upon them a barrage of harassment and certain acts of economic reprisal. By September 1964 none of the Heffners (there were two daughters in the family) was a resident of McComb, and it is not exaggerating the case to say that their departure was prompted by fear of physical injury, or even death.

Carter makes clear his opinion that the Heffners' predicament, suffering, and fate equalled, in miniature, the violent throes suffered by the small town of McComb as it grappled with the dilemma of unyielding tradition challenged by implacable change. He writes:

At the beginning of the summer of 1964, McComb was a community hag-ridden by fear, fear of a skirmish line of Northern students coming

to spread foolish notions about civil rights and to plant seeds of insur-
rection in the heads of the good darkies of the city and Pike County and
Southwest Mississippi; fear of the federal government and the all-
seeing agents of the Federal Bureau of Investigation; fear of what might
happen next anywhere; fear of the Ku Klux Klan; fear of economic
disaster for the individual and for the town. . . . Through the long days
and longer nights most of the people of McComb mourned, but not
openly, over the bombings and the burnings and the beatings which
destroyed the once attractive image of their town. The perpetrators
were but a handful. But those who did nothing about it made up, until
the leaves of autumn began to fall, all but a tiny fraction of the
citizenry. The Heffners' tragedy was a personal one. The larger tragedy
and the shame of it were McComb's.[10]

Carter also declares that the Heffners served a certain function:
they "became the scapegoats for a community's hysteria, bigotry,
ignorance, cowardice, and fear, which in time of unfamiliar stress
form a scum which hides whatever bubbles cleanly in the human
cauldron."[11] In other words, they bore the brunt, at least partially,
of the community's inability to cope with the change-tradition confrontation.

The Heffners' fate was tragic, but so was the fate of tradition-
bound McComb. We know, however, that tragedy offers us, in
addition to pity and fear, catharsis, a purgation of those emotions.
So the Heffners Left McComb, published in 1965, can only hint at
such purgation. Carter's last chapter outlines McComb's effort to
come to grips with the situation, an effort spearheaded by a series
of editorials in the McComb *Enterprise-Journal* in the fall of 1964.
The fruit of this effort was the apprehension of a number of sus-
pected bombers and night-riders and the drafting, in the form of a
petition, of a community statement of principles. Carter, writing
during the last acts of the tragedy, can only conclude with these
words: "It would be pleasant to end with praise for a community's
catharsis. But although brighter days may lie ahead for Pike
County, there may yet be other flame-bright nights."[12]

J. O. Emmerich's *Two Faces of Janus* continues, in a certain
respect, the story Hodding Carter started. Although a fair amount
of the book deals with earlier history, a substantial portion of it
focuses on the conflict of the 1960s, and so it deserves a place in
this account. The final chapters of the book recount the responsible
actions Emmerich undertook, through his position as editor of the

McComb *Enterprise-Journal*, to pacify Pike County following the summer of 1964. In chapters titled "'Go to Jail First'," "Reign of Terror," and "The Sheriff's Request" Emmerich outlines the events leading to the clash of change and tradition and the fledgling efforts of McComb to move from a position of intransigent tradition. Several of his editorials, in whole or part, are reprinted; their burden is an earnest pleading for "citizens to join in a responsible effort to return [the] city to normalcy."[13] Emmerich tells his newspaper's readers that the "time is here to move the McComb community into a new era of responsibility."[14] These are the opening words of the most important editorial, one that, in Emmerich's words, "pleaded, begged, implored in an effort to halt the divorce proceedings the McComb community was waging against reality."[15] "Soon thereafter," says Emmerich, "a spark of hope was ignited."[16]

Two Faces of Janus also deserves a place among these books because it carries us beyond the troubled early years of the decade. The book was published in 1973, giving Emmerich the advantage of some perspective. In the book's final chapter, "The Road to Damascus," Emmerich assesses the situation eight years after the "long hot summer" and declares that "colossal changes have come to pass in a short time."[17] Emmerich writes with a dose of heady optimism, one not always borne out by subsequent events. But the fact that he was able to be so bold is, to some extent, supportive of his assessment of the changes wrought. Emmerich speaks of "a new day dawning": "Across the Deep South—in Georgia and Alabama, in South Carolina and Arkansas, in Mississippi and Louisiana—the cottonpatch philosophy is yielding to the forces of enlightenment. A thousand Deep South communities can make this testimony. And they boast of it."[18] He calls upon "people outside the Deep South" to recognize "this epochal change. They should not err," he continues,

> by thinking of yesterday and calling it today. They may continue to think of the Deep South that was and not grasp the reality of the Deep South that is. There is a human tendency to think and live in the past. Thus it is difficult for people to recognize the new viewpoints and new patterns which other persons have accepted.[19]

Finally, he asserts "that the changes in the Deep South in recent years represent something resembling a miracle":

The New South today is coming alive because southern people at long last are manifesting a willingness to come face to face with reality. Comparatively few Americans across the nation are aware of this historic breakthrough. Fewer still recognize the reason for this spectacular achievement.

The difference between the Old South and the New South is primarily a difference in the attitudes of the people. The willingness of some, the reluctance of others, to abandon concepts which conflict with the Constitution of our country—these attitudes mark the division and are the reason for the delay in the fruition of a New South. What has happened to create this New South is an unknown factor to many Americans today. But today a New South is in the process of being born. The evidence of it can be seen in the new thinking and feeling of the people.[20]

As I have suggested, Emmerich is overly optimistic. But his book does serve to carry us through the clash, and it helps us to begin to focus on the outcome of the change-tradition conflict.

The fifth book in this half-dozen is Willie Morris's *Yazoo: Integration in a Deep-Southern Town*. Published in 1971, it chronicles Morris's several trips to his hometown, Yazoo City, throughout 1970. These trips were undertaken for the purpose of observing the town's experience with full-scale school integration as mandated by the *Alexander v. Holmes* decision of 1969. Morris's book is thoughtful and well-written, and its main burden is, once again, the monumental clash of change and tradition. Here, for example, is Morris's assessment of the fifteen years from 1955 through 1969; although he concentrates on Yazoo City, he points out that events there were "similar to what happened throughout the state":

> There were a few weak glimmers of a new awareness, the stirring of the blacks under the example of Martin Luther King, the faith among them in the ideal of a truly just and integrated society, the gradual halting movement of the whole federal authority through the courts, through Kennedy and Johnson and voting-rights laws toward some dramatic thrust. But by and large among the whites the failure of leadership, symbolized in the Meredith fiasco at Ole Miss in 1962 and the violence of the '64 summer, was so profound as to border on the tragic.[21]

But by early 1970 intransigent tradition had begun to weaken; "all over town," says Morris, "were suggestions that something new was coming to the surface . . . something never quite articulated with any degree of force or with the courage of numbers in many

Deep-Southern towns, some painful summoning from deepest wellsprings."[22]

As the change-tradition clash began to play itself out in the desegration of a small-town school system, Morris began to perceive the impact of what was happening. He writes:

> But from the old surfaces, from the immemorial orders of life, something ironic and momentous was slowly emerging. An immense facade was beginning to crack, barely perceptible at first, but to a writer and a son of Mississippi, it was the little things which were gradually enclosing and symbolizing the promise and the magnitude of what might be taking place here. If a true human revolution implies the basic restructuring of everyday life, the essential patterns of behavior toward other people, then what might be occurring here was a revolution, subtle and intensely complicated.[23]

Morris, like Emmerich, ends his book on an optimistic note, but Morris's optimism is tempered; his conclusions are more guarded, his insights more profound than are Emmerich's. And his ability as a writer far surpasses that of Emmerich. These observations are clearly supported, I believe, by Morris's final sentences on change and tradition in Yazoo City:

> I believe that what happens in a small Mississippi town with less of a population than three or four apartment complexes on the West Side of Manhattan Island will be of enduring importance to America. It is people trying: loving, hating, enduring cruelties and perpetrating them, all caught, exacerbated, and dramatized by our brighter and darker impulses. Its best instincts only barely carried the day, and still may fall before anything really gets started (for we are mature enough in our failures by now to know how thin is the skein of our civilization), but nonetheless these instincts responded in ways that served us all. How many other little towns in America would have done nearly so well? Southerners of both races share a rootedness that even in moments of anger and pain we have been unable to repudiate or ignore, for the South—all of what it is—is in us all. . . . One of the burdens of the people of all the Yazoos who share this place and this involvement in a common history—a history of anguish and cruelty and inhumanity, but also of courage and warmth and rare hospitality—is to warn their fellow Americans of the terrible toll that bitterness and retreat can take; for this will give the nation some feel of itself, and help it to endure.[24]

The final book to be considered in this essay, Florence Mars's *Witness in Philadelphia*, returns us to the summer of 1964. As the title indicates, the book is concerned with the disappearance of Michael Schwerner, James Chaney, and Andrew Goodman. But the book is much more than an account of the perpetration and solution of a heinous crime. Mars probes deeply into the tradition that set the stage for the murder; she also probes her community's collective psyche, as well as her own. Her book contains a fairly lengthy description of her life before 1964—"As I was growing up," she writes, "I saw [the] world I lived in as a very well-ordered and generally uncomplicated place"[25]—in addition to a long account of the civil-rights workers' disappearance and its aftermath and a brief discussion, from her perspective in 1977, of the outcome of the change-tradition confrontation of the 1960s.

Florence Mars's witnessing is powerful. Her writing is sober, even somber, as we might expect from the topic she addresses. *Witness in Philadelphia* provides a needed counterpointing of Emmerich's optimistic projections and Morris's rhapsodic hopes. For example, assessing the situation in 1972, she writes:

> Two years after the trial ended, the climate had changed in Neshoba County. No longer could one yell "civil rights" and "outside interference," as had once been possible, and mold resistance to almost anything. The confrontation had taken place; emotions reached an intensity that was difficult to recall, and men were waiting to go to prison for their part in putting three "integrationists" underneath twenty feet of dirt.[26]

But, she adds later, "Ten years after the trial, the case is almost never discussed, and when it is there is evidence of dilemma. It cannot be said that the community has collectively confronted the facts of the Neshoba case, let alone the responsibility. . . ."[27] She also aserts, however, that "there can be no question that the community has learned from the experience, at the least, the supremely difficult lesson of defeat."[28] *Witness in Philadelphia* ends with a description of the dedication of a commemorative monument in 1976. Mars's account blends elements of change and tradition, and points up the effects of both, in a few well-chosen, weighty words. She concludes: "But the people—black and white—who met at Mt. Nebo Baptist Church on December 12, 1976, are not mute. They spoke and the monument they erected in memory of James Chaney, Michael Schwerner, and Andrew Goodman will continue to speak for them, with them, of them."[29]

What is the message of these six accounts of small towns caught in the throes of change and tradition? They are, all of them, testimonies of turmoil, travail, trouble. Each book speaks of people, people in small towns, people who could not easily escape to some comfortable suburb or impersonal high-rise. Instead, they had to resolve the change-tradition confrontation on the squares and main streets of their towns. There was nowhere to run, and the crises would not simply go away.

If we retreat for a moment from these six books and listen to other voices, voices that act as a commentary on the books, I think the message will become clear. In 1963 James Silver wrote, "The long-run future of Mississippi not only looks promising but is inevitably alluring. As for the short run, the next ten years, we are in for bitter strife and really deep trouble."[30] In the following year the Kosciusko (Mississippi) *Star-Herald* declared forthrightly that "it's time we change, or be destroyed by change."[31] In 1965 Silver closed his essay "Revolution Begins in the Closed Society" with a powerful observation on change and tradition:

> In a closed and sick society the crisis has been met and passed. What Mississippians now face is a long period of controlled convalescence. The possibility of relapse cannot be denied. The effort at understanding and change that thousands upon thousands of conventional white segregationists will have to make will be enormous. The effort Negroes shall have to continue and enlarge passeth understanding. What is required of all Mississippians is nothing short of the transformation of the traditions and social structure of a settled and outmoded society. The stakes are high and the margin for error thin. No honest student of Mississippi's long past and recent history could fail to agree, however, that its prospects for genuine democracy have never been better. The day will yet come when Mississippi not only accepts the end of segregation but welcomes and embraces integration simply because it is right.[32]

A decade and more after "the long hot summer" it was obvious that the clash of change and tradition had created, as these earlier voices had foreseen, a new reality. David Donald, Harvard professor, native Mississippian, assessed the traditional situation in the South (and, therefore, in Mississippi) in this way:

> All of us know that there is not one South; there are at least two. One of these Souths is a land of violence and hatred. This is the South where whites kept blacks in slavery for more than two centuries and then held

them in segregated serfdom, in some ways more degrading than slavery, for another hundred years. This is the South where the farmers raped the land, the factory owners squeezed their mill operators, and the planters cheated their tenants. This is the South that is thin in culture, suspicious in outlook, and bigoted in ideas. . . .

But there is another South. I do not invoke images of magnolia-shaded plantations, where young gallants rode to the foxes, cheered on by damsels in hoops and crinolines. . . . That South never existed outside of fiction. But there is, and there always has been, a real South of basic goodness and decency, whose inhabitants, black as well as white, have a deep sense of attachment to place, a strong feeling of kinship, and a profound belief in their God. This is the South that is a land of frankness and openness, a land of generosity and courtesy.[33]

Commenting on Donald's words, Charles Sallis, author of the aptly titled *Mississippi: Conflict and Change,* advanced his hopes that Mississippi, having learned from its experiences with change and tradition, could play a new role. He wrote:

The South, including Mississippi, seems to me to be at a kind of crossroads. We live in an age in which nationally there appears to be a loss of purpose, an erosion of confidence and a decline in the feeling of sense of community. Southerners of all races seem to have a unique sense of time and place, of belonging, of community, no matter how tough the times have been. Perhaps we can lead the nation in finding its lost purpose and restoring its confidence and sense of community. Perhaps that is our mission and our purpose. Perhaps that is Mississippi's role in the nation. Maybe the prodigal daughter can lead the way.[34]

And Roy Hudson, speaking in 1978, succinctly and eloquently summed up his observations on change and tradition: "Let those of us who have insight into the realities of the past and the progress of the future commit ourselves to helping bring about one common view of hope and prosperity for all Mississippians."[35]

The message rings, I think, loud and clear. Intransigent tradition leads only to desperation and difficulty. But the reverse situation is likewise: unheeding change also brings desperation and difficulty. My discipline, literature, furnishes numerous examples of this truth. Shirley Jackson's classic story "The Lottery" speaks to the point. So, too, do Robert Frost's lines from "Mending Wall": "He moves in darkness as it seems to me . . . / He will not go behind his father's saying. . . ."[36] And W. B. Yeats's lament for Ireland (surely a prime example of the collision of change and tradition) seems chillingly appropriate:

Hearts with one purpose alone
Through summer and winter seem
Enchanted to a stone. . . .
Too long a sacrifice
Can make a stone of the heart.[37]

Small towns—in Mississippi, in Montana, in this country—must heed the demands of *both* change and tradition. If they do, they are in a compelling position to provide the insights and answers that will lead to a better life for all. The six books I have discussed in this essay bear witness—sometimes heart-breaking, sometimes exhilarating—to that truth.

NOTES

[1] C. Hugh Holman, "The Southerner as American Writer," in *The Roots of Southern Writing: Essays on the Literature of the American South* (Athens: University of Georgia Press, 1972), p. 1.

[2] James W. Silver, Pref., *Letters from Mississippi*, ed. Elizabeth Sutherland (1965; rpt. New York: New American Library, 1966), p. ix.

[3] Anne Moody, *Coming of Age in Mississippi* (1968; rpt. New York: Dell, 1980), p. 366.

[4] Moody, p. 384.   [5] Moody, p. 384.

[6] Elizabeth Sutherland, ed., *Letters from Mississippi* (1965; rpt. New York: New American Library, 1966), p. 49.

[7] Sutherland, p. 211.   [8] Sutherland, p. 211.

[9] Hodding Carter, *So the Heffners Left McComb* (Garden City, New York: Doubleday, 1965), p. 9.

[10] Carter, pp. 66–67.   [11] Carter, p. 88.   [12] Carter, pp. 141–142.

[13] J. Oliver Emmerich, *Two Faces of Janus: The Saga of Deep South Change* (Jackson: University and College Press of Mississippi, 1973), p. 138.

[14] Emmerich, p. 138.   [15] Emmerich, p. 141.   [16] Emmerich, p. 141.

[17] Emmerich, p. 151.   [18] Emmerich, p. 154.   [19] Emmerich, p. 155.

[20] Emmerich, pp. 157–158.

[21] Willie Morris, *Yazoo: Integration in a Deep-Southern Town* (New York: Harper & Row, 1971), p. 19.

[22] Morris, p. 33.   [23] Morris, p. 133.   [24] Morris, pp. 191–192.

[25] Florence Mars, *Witness in Philadelphia* (Baton Rogue: Louisiana State University Press, 1977), p. 41.

[26] Mars, p. 269.   [27] Mars, p. 271.

[28] Mars, p. 272.   [29] Mars, p. 281.

[30] James W. Silver, *Mississippi: The Closed Society*, new ed. (New York: Harcourt, Brace & World, 1966), p. 229.

[31] Billy McMillan, as quoted in Silver, *Mississippi*, p. 296.

[32] Silver, *Mississippi*, pp. 365–366.

[33] David Donald, as quoted in Charles Sallis, "Images of Mississippi," in *Sense of Place: Mississippi*, ed. Peggy W. Prenshaw and Jesse O. McKee (Jackson: University Press of Mississippi, 1979), p. 69.

[34] Sallis, p. 69.

[35] Roy Hudson, "Mississippi: A Native View," in *Sense of Place: Mississippi*, p. 64.

[36] Robert Frost, *Selected Poems of Robert Frost* (New York: Holt, Rinehart and Winston, 1963), p. 24.

[37] W. B. Yeats, *The Collected Poems of W. B. Yeats* (New York: Macmillan, 1956), p. 179.

Family Life in Small Towns and Rural Communities:

Persistence, Change and Diversity

RAYMOND T. COWARD

Preliminary data from the 1980 Census have indicated that the urban-to-rural migrational shift that began to be tracked in the early 1970s has continued into this decade. In all regions of the nation, except the South, the rate of nonmetropolitan growth in the 1970s exceeded that of metropolitan areas.[1]

In addition to the significance of this trend for demographers—it ends decades of rural-to-urban migration—it is interesting to family sociologists as well because, if certain scholars are correct, the impetus for this trend is voluntary and apparently not, as with most population shifts, a result of economic hardship, political persecution, famine, or perceived opportunities for prosperity.[2]

Although there is not complete homogeneity in the motives of the migrants, nor in their goals or values, it does appear that a large majority of the inmigrants are willing to sacrifice career development and economic gains for what they perceive as a better environment in which to lead their lives.[3] A commitment to family life is often a major dimension of this decision. Rural communities are seen as healthy environments for child rearing and for enhancing marital and family relationships. Unfortunately, the validity of these assumptions has not been widely researched and data from longitudinal studies of family adjustments to rural migration are lacking.[4]

More and more sociologists are focusing their attention on the family in rural society because this "new wave" of urban immigrants is added to an already significantly large stable rural population.[5] Much of the recent popular and professional debate about rural families has centered on whether rural families are becoming more like urban families. Some have argued that the stark differences between the city and the country have been reduced by an "urbanization" trend or that the influence and pervasiveness of the

73

mass media have created a more homogeneous society.[6] In contrast, others insist that there are still sufficient spatial, environmental and attitudinal differences between urban and rural communities to continue to consider them as distinct entities.[7]

Actually, there is evidence for the accuracy of both conclusions. Many of the characteristics that urban families exhibit have parallels in families who reside in small towns and rural communities. At the same time, rural families continue to be significantly *different* from urban families in many socio-economic characteristics and interpersonal processes. Coward has suggested that "it is as if rural and urban families are riding parallel but different roads . . . heading in the same direction but remaining on separate paths."[8] Carlson, Lassey and Lassey have asserted that "the difference between rural and urban communities is more a matter of rapidity and degree than of change versus nonchange."[9]

Persistence, change and *diversity* are three key concepts that scholars have used to organize sociological knowledge about the lives of families in small-town America.[10] At first these concepts may appear to be contradictory, unable to reflect simultaneously the internal dynamics of the same families. Yet, if we penetrate surface appearances and peel away layers of folklore, repeated observations will indicate not only that the three concepts are present and operative but, more importantly, that each provides useful insights into the complex dynamics of family life in small towns and rural America. These three concepts are considered separately below and their ability to characterize the modern rural family is illustrated.

Persistence

Research has established that there are persistent differences between the structural family characteristics of rural and urban families, and between their attitudes toward family relationships, economic conditions, and the function of family life. These trends can be illustrated by the following:

Structural Family Characteristics: Analyzing census data from 1950 to 1970, Brown concluded that there continued to be significant rural-urban differences in family structure. His analyses, for example, indicate that rural residents continued to

. . . marry earlier than their urban counterparts, have more children, and live in larger households. Labor force participation continues to be lower among rural women, and a smaller proportion of rural marriages end in divorce.[11]

Although the data from the 1980 Census were not available when Brown completed his analyses, there is little reason to believe that these persistent differences, spanning more than three decades, will suddenly evaporate. We may witness a narrowing of the gap in certain structural characteristics, such as we notice in the converging rates of fertility; in general, though, many statistically and pragmatically significant differences will continue to distinguish urban family lives from those of rural residents.

Attitudes Toward Family Relationships: Larson's analyses of data from Gallup Polls have documented ongoing and significant differences between rural and urban attitudes regarding marriage, family, and related issues.[12] For example, residents of rural communities are more likely to believe that (1) premarital sex is wrong; (2) birth control pills should not be available to teenage girls; (3) abortion should not be legalized; and (4) divorce should be made more difficult to obtain.

However, the rural-urban comparisons that have been reported by pollsters and researchers may actually underestimate the true differences that exist because most research fails to take into account the community of origin of each respondent. Carlson, Lassey and Lassey have posited that the "size of community of origin is a better predictor of attitudes and behavior than is the current residence."[13] Since others have estimated that as much as one-quarter to one-half of the current urban adult community grew up in rural America,[14] comparisons of current residents may mask the true magnitude of the cultural discrepancies that persist between rural and urban communities.

The lack of long-term comparative data severely restricts the ability to judge whether the rural-urban attitudinal differences that now exist are larger or smaller than those of previous generations. Brown restated the "separate but parallel paths" analogy in a different form when he argued that, with reference to Gallup Poll data, "attitudinal data seem to suggest a persistence of rural-urban differentiation as well as a continuity of change."[15]

Economic Conditions: Sociologists generally accept the well-documented evidence of the close and substantial influence of economic conditions on the internal dynamics and functioning of the family. The effects of poverty, for example, have been shown to be devastating to the family, taking their toll in personal and interpersonal disruption and strife. What is less understood, by the general public and by many academicians, is how large a proportion of rural people live under poverty conditions. Too often poverty is considered an urban problem, one that haunts the back alleys and tenement houses of our inner cities. In terms of absolute numbers this is an accurate portrait; yet it ignores, or at least reduces, the significance of the following:

- more than 2 million rural families remained below the poverty level in 1978; 7 percent of those were farm families;[16]
- nearly 40 percent of all poor people in the United States lived in nonmetropolitan areas in 1970;[17] and,
- in 1976, 38 percent of rural black families were considered poor and 28 percent of rural Hispanic families had annual incomes below $6000.[18]

The incidence of rural poverty has decreased dramatically in the last decade; yet it remains a disproportionate share of the total poverty in our nation. Furthermore, this poverty is often associated with chronically depressed rural areas and, existing throughout entire regions, can affect several generations of the same family. Some sociologists believe that the value and belief systems that emerge in such cultures can serve to perpetuate poverty by providing a false sense of well-being and security for the family while encouraging acceptance and compliance.[19]

Many think of the rural poor as less disadvantaged than their urban counterparts. Popular images show them as supplementing their meager resources by raising big gardens to feed their children, chopping wood to heat their homes, and catching fish in the local pond or creek to provide protein. Nonsense! More often than not, such activities are desperate attempts by the poor to "make do" and are not adequate substitutes for a stable and prosperous economic environment. Poor is poor—and if anything, because it's not very visible to the general public, rural poverty may be a double jeopardy.

Functional Properties: Finally, despite many predictions to the contrary, the family persists as a relatively stable unit and continues to be the preeminent force in the process of socialization. This does not mean that changes have not occurred; they have. But these changes have altered little the most basic functions of the family, to provide love and protection and to establish an environment for growth.

Furthermore, family sociologists have witnessed a recent change in focus that is very encouraging to many of us in the field—a greater recognition of, and respect for, the *strengths* of families.[20] Rural families today are experiencing unprecedented stress; yet most families are responding in constructive, healthy ways that reinforce their importance.[21] As we learn more about what characterizes strong families, we begin to appreciate that these underlying dimensions can assume many different structures and forms. Careful studies of rural families must not confuse changes in structure with changes in function.

When we acknowledge that rural families have been characterized by persistence, we must not imprudently generalize these observations. Persistence is just *one* part of the complex puzzle that characterizes the dynamics of rural family life. Without the other pieces—change and diversity—we are left with a distorted impression of reality. As William M. Smith and I have warned, the

> . . . image of the family in rural society must not be frozen in 'still life' forms, like a Grandma Moses painting or a Currier and Ives print. The family in rural society would be more accurately characterized as the "family-in-process" or the "family becoming."[22]

Change is a part of the lives of all rural families—changes in themselves, in their homes and in the communities in which they live. I have suggested elsewhere "a changing rural society is affecting the family—and the changing family is affecting rural society."[23]

Change

Family sociologists have been very much interested in documenting and exploring changes in rural families. Here are some illustrations of the changes that have been observed:

Structural Changes: Brown describes some of the structural changes in rural families that have occurred over the past quarter of a century.[24] From his analyses of census data from 1950 to 1970, he concluded that there were clear trends toward rural couples delaying marriage until they were older, choosing to have fewer children, and living in smaller households. He also documented increases in the rate of divorce among rural families and the number of women employed outside the home. In particular, this increase in the number of rural women employed outside the home, perhaps one of the most significant changes that have occurred in rural families, has a profound potential for influencing the daily living routines of families.[25] In the 1970s the participation of rural women in the labor force increased by 53 percent—4.5 million rural women! By 1980, it is estimated, 48 percent of all nonmetropolitan women were employed.[26]

Most family sociologists routinely accept the existence of structural changes in rural families and expect that these trends will continue into the near future. They lack, however, a thorough understanding of how these changes affect the internal dynamics and daily lifestyles of the rural family.[27] Although it is important to document the existence and magnitude of the changes, it is perhaps more important to appreciate the "meaning" of these changes in the rural context. I have expressed this shortcoming in another study, cautioning that the

> . . . changes that rural families experience occur in a psychosocial, or attitudinal, environment that is consistently different from urban society. Rural America is not simply a smaller scale urban setting. Rural America is qualitatively different and unique from metropolitan America. Because of these contextual differences, we must be cautious about assuming that the same general trend in families holds identical, or even similar, meanings in the two environments. The direction of change is important, the magnitude of change is important; but, ultimately the impact of change on individuals and families will, in large part, be determined by the meaning attached by the community to the change.[28]

Social-Service Changes: At the time of the initiation of the "Great Society" programs of the 1960s, the problems of our inner cities were front-page headlines, and rioting in the streets was a reality. Thus, programs designed to bring about social improvement reflected a distinct urban bias and were best suited for urban implementation. Political and academic debate raged over which strategy offered the best possible solution to the turmoil of the cities. National energies and fiscal resources were mobilized and directed toward reversing the "decaying" social and economic trend of inner-city family life. Social planners soon realized, however, that the city programs did nothing for a large number of families and individuals living in sparsely populated areas. Concurrently, sociologists realized that some of the social problems that were infecting the big city were also happening "down on the farm." Data emerged to suggest that

- many rural public schools provided inadequate educations for their students;[29]
- alcoholism was a problem of significant proportions for small towns and rural communities;[30]
- many rural elderly persons lived in deplorable conditions and were seriously disadvantaged when compared to their urban and suburban counterparts;[31] and
- rural populations experienced high rates of mental health problems; yet the availability of practitioners and supportive facilities was severely limited.[32]

Collectively these realizations have resulted in a substantial growth of nonmetropolitan social services, and certain types of services—gerontological services, for example—may have grown *more* in rural America.[33] Yet this change has not eradicated the rural-urban differences in the range and number of services available for families and individuals in crisis.[34] Recognizing the inadequacies of urban service models for small towns, some authors have called for innovative programs specifically designed for rural implementation.[35] In addition, others are attempting to refine and articulate the dimensions of needs in rural mental-health and family services.[36] These efforts are important first steps which will begin to define strategies and models and to identify the skills, attitudes and knowledge needed for the successful implementation of rural services. "Until such an empirical basis is built, rural social service delivery will too often be haphazard and serendipitous."[37]

Economic and Community Changes: Finally, the context and

environment in which families exist have been altered. For many years "rural" was synonymous with "agricultural" in our country, but that characterization is no longer accurate. Most rural families today are *not* farm families. The Department of Agriculture (USDA) has indicated that "in 1979, the most recent year for which final data was available, about 6.2 million persons were living on farms. . . . Put another way, only one of every 33 persons—3 percent of the nation's 220 million—resided on a farm."[38] Remember, the total rural population in 1980 topped sixty-two million— one out of every four persons! Only about ten percent of the current *rural* population lives on farms.

After an exhaustive national review of the current structure of American agriculture, the USDA concluded:

"When we look anew at rural America after the experience of the past decade, we could not help but be struck by the magnitude of the changes that have transformed the rural economy and rural communities in the United States. As farm production and earnings have continued to become more concentrated into fewer and larger units, the rural non-farm economy has grown and diversified in ways that have had profound implications for farmers, especially small farm operators and their families; for other rural residents, and for rural communities."[39]

Illustrating the changing structure of agriculture, Wilkening discussed the rapidly growing trend toward off-farm employment by males. While employment off-farm was once considered a transitional phase either into or out of farming, Wilkening suggested that it may now be a more permanent pattern for many farm families, a means for those "who wish to retain farming as their primary occupation but require additional income to pay farm debts or to add to family income."[40]

The shift away from farming has resulted in other industrial enterprises for rural communities. The USDA has reported that of the "13 million jobs created nationally between 1970 and 1977, more than 40 percent were located in nonmetropolitan areas."[41] These new employment opportunities represent a wide range of occupations (see the later section on economic diversity) and result in a substantially different rural labor market from that which existed a decade ago.

Sometimes this development has come slowly, allowing communities to anticipate the changes and plan for them well in advance. In other instances, the growth has come more rapidly, with changes coming ahead of proper planning. The energy "boom towns" of the West and the Northwest are perhaps the most vivid examples of rural communities thrust suddenly into a rapidly changing economic and cultural vortex.[42]

The rural environment has been further changed by the arrival of inmigrants from more urban environments. As noted in 1980, the "influx of outsiders, flatlanders, city folks and easterners has transformed rural America into a pluralistic mosaic of our entire country."[43] Many people believe that this plurality of lifestyles has strengthened and enriched the family life of our small towns. However, this diversity has also destroyed for many Americans their simplistic notion of the mystical rural farm family. Diversity is alive and well and living in rural America!

Diversity

In the zeal to focus attention on the importance of rural issues, practitioners, politicians and academicians have sometimes obfuscated the diversity that exists in the all-inclusive category we call "rural."[44] It is easy to lose sight of the fact that we are concerned with a very wide variety of patterns, each one of long continuity where it is found—at one extreme New York City, Los Angeles and Chicago and at the other such places as Thunder Hawk, South Dakota; Red Lick, Mississippi, and Wallagrass, Maine. The limitations of creating a rural/urban dichotomy are considered elsewhere;[45] it is sufficient to note here that social scientists and policymakers interested in rural problems in the 1980s need to be sensitive to the various types of diversity that exist. Some of the forms of that diversity are explored here.

Ethnic Diversity: Rural America has always been a rich and varied mix of ethnic and cultural heritages.[46] A sample of this plurality is reflected in the work of Hawkes, Kutner, Wells, Christopherson and Almirol on the rural families of black, Mexican-American, Navajo and Filipino descent.[47] But this list only begins to suggest the full range of ethnic diversity, which embraces the Scotch-Irish, Dutch, German and Scandinavian settlements of the forest and lake country of Michigan, Wisconsin, and Minnesota;

the Franco-Americans in Northern New England; the Cajuns in southern Louisiana; and the Eskimos in Alaska. Each of these groups has permanently embossed its heritage and customs on the countryside of rural America, and with the "recent influx of immigrants from Asia and Cuba the diversity of family life in rural America seems not to be waning."[48] It would be inaccurate and misleading to ignore the existence of this ethnic diversity in discussions of national policy or debates about the character of rural communities.

Regional and Geographic Diversity: Similarly, to ignore the enormous natural land variations that exist among rural regions in our country is like ignoring the essential differences between apples and oranges merely because they both fall into the category of fruits. Small towns and rural communities in America are alike in many ways, but they are not carbon copies of one another. Comprehensive analyses remind us that rural communities display differences as great as those among the quaintness of small New England fishing towns, the immensity of sheep and cattle ranches in the West and Southwest, the cosmopolitanism of the California wine valleys and the serenity of the hills and back hollows of Appalachia.

Recently, some provocative studies by Peter L. Heller and his colleagues have attempted to illustrate how different familial forms are associated with specific regions of the country.[49] Although their work remains highly controversial, it does emphasize that the significant geographical variations among rural regions in our country may have important implications for the way in which families conduct their lives and interact with their kin, friends and neighbors, and, that geographical factors may determine the resources that a region has available to call on in times of crisis.

Diversity in Economic Development: The economic and developmental prosperity that some small towns have enjoyed has not been equally shared by all rural areas. In an analysis of thirteen nonmetropolitan areas in nine Northeastern states, researchers were able to classify areas as either declining, stable or expanding, on the basis of changes in family income and population between 1960 and 1970.[50] Surveys conducted in sample communities from these areas disclosed significant relationships between a commu-

nity's decline, stability, or expansion and various factors including
(1) the dependency ratio of the community; (2) the education and
income of the residents; (3) the years of residence in the areas;
(4) the availability of municipal water and sewer lines; and (5) the
satisfaction with community services. The authors suggested that
"The differences between declining, stable and expanding communities are fundamental and raise important community-
development-policy questions about state and national support and
aid for community facilities and services."[51]

Where rural regions are characterized by growth and economic
development, such prosperity is not necessarily universal or
equally distributed to all towns or to all segments of the society. As
a black economic development worker has commented, "There are
some shady spots in the Sun Belt."[52] Poor families and the most
economically depressed rural communities are most often the last
to share in the new-found wealth of a region.

Employment Diversity: As I have mentioned, rural America is no
longer synonymous with agriculture. By 1977 there were almost
three times as many factory workers as farm workers in rural
America.[53] These same data indicated the proportionally small
fraction of the rural labor market that was employed in farming
activities including forestry and fisheries—8.6% in 1977. In contrast, the largest sources of rural employment were (1) service
jobs—29.9%; (2) manufacturing—22.6%; and (3) retail trade—
16.9%.[54] Nearly seven out of every ten rural workers were employed in one of these three areas.

Each of these forms of diversity—ethnic, regional, economic and
employment—serves to destroy the simplistic, uniform picture of
rural America. Diversity is one of the basic threads of the rural
fabric that serves to shape family life.

Conclusion

When used to organize sociological understandings about the family in rural society, the concepts of persistence, change, and diversity collectively capture the essence of many of the trends that are
simultaneously emerging and converging in the lives of families in
small-town America. To summarize our current state of knowledge:

- We *know* that the nonmetropolitan population in America is growing.

- We *know* that rural America has undergone significant and rapid changes in the last quarter of a century and that these changes can affect the quality of family life.

- We *know* that many families in rural society are experiencing severe and critical problems of an economic, interpersonal, individual and familial nature.

- We *know* that supportive services for families are fewer and narrower in range in nonmetropolitan America.

- Yet we continue to have an *inadequate understanding* of the impact of all of these, and of other trends not touched on here, on sustaining and enhancing the quality of life for families in rural America.[55]

NOTES

[1] Calvin L. Beale, *Rural and Small Town Population Change, 1970–80*, ESS-5 (Washington, D.C.: U.S. Department of Agriculture, Economics and Statistics Service, February, 1981), pp. 1–4. Even though this migrational reversal is significant, its magnitude must be kept in perspective. Certain locales are exceptions, but, nationally, the majority of people who lived in small towns and rural communities at the time of the 1980 Census also lived in such environments a decade before.

[2] Louis A. Ploch, "The Reversal of Migration Patterns: Some Rural Development Consequences," *Rural Sociology*, 43 (1978), 293–303.

[3] Louis A. Ploch, "Maine's New Pattern of Inmigration: Some Significance and Consequences," University of Maine—Orono, Department of Agricultural and Resource Economics, 1976.

[4] Louis A. Ploch, "Family Aspects of the New Wave of Inmigrants to Rural Communities," in *The Family in Rural Society*, ed. Raymond T. Coward and William M. Smith, Jr. (Boulder, Colorado: Westview Press, 1981), pp. 39–53; Raymond T. Coward and William M. Smith, Jr., "Families in Rural Society," in *Rural Society: Issues for the 1980s*, ed. Don A. Dillman and Daryl J. Hobbs (Boulder, Colorado: Westview Press, 1982), pp. 77–84.

[5] Coward and Smith, eds., *The Family in Rural Society*; Coward and Smith, "Families in Rural Society."

[6] Paul C. Rosenblatt, A. Nevaldine and S. L. Titus, "Farm Families: Relation of Significant Attributes of Farming to Family Interaction," *International Journal of Sociology of the Family*, 9 (1978), 89–99; T. L. Smith and P. E. Zopf, Jr., *Principles of Inductive Rural Sociology* (Philadelphia: F. A. Davis, 1970).

[7] William M. Smith, Jr. and Raymond T. Coward, "The Family in Rural Society: Images of the Future," in *The Family in Rural Society*, ed. Coward and Smith, pp. 221–229.

[8] Raymond T. Coward, "Demythologizing the Farm Family," *Catholic Rural Life*, 31, no. 1 (1981), 18.

[9] J. E. Carlson, Marie L. Lassey and William R. Lassey, *Rural Society and Environment in America* (New York: McGraw-Hill Book Company, 1981), p. 60.

[10] Thomas R. Ford, ed., *Rural U.S.A.: Persistence and Change* (Ames, Iowa: Iowa State University Press, 1978).

[11] David L. Brown, "A Quarter Century of Trends and Changes in the Demographic Structure of American Families," in *The Family in Rural Society*, ed. Coward and Smith, pp. 9–25.

[12] Olaf F. Larson, "Values and Beliefs of Rural People," in *Rural U.S.A.: Persistence and Change*, ed. Thomas R. Ford (Ames, Iowa: Iowa State University Press, 1978).

[13] Carlson, Lassey and Lassey, *Rural Society*, p. 66.

[14] Norval Glenn and L. Hill, Jr., "Rural-Urban Differences in Attitudes and Behavior in the United States," *The Annals of the American Academy of Political and Social Science*, 429 (1977), 36–50.

[15] Brown, "A Quarter Century of Trends," p. 16.

[16] U.S. Department of Agriculture, *A Time to Choose: Summary Report on the Structure of Agriculture*, Publication No. 723-560-686 (Washington, D.C.: U.S. Government Printing Office, 1981).

[17] Carlson, Lassey and Lassey, *Rural Society*.

[18] Irma T. Elo, "The Changing Rural Economy," *Rural Community Development*, 3, no. 1 (1981), 1–8. (Published and distributed by the National Rural Center, Washington, D.C.).

[19] Janet M. Fitchen, *Poverty in Rural America: A Case Study* (Boulder, Colorado: Westview Press, 1981).

[20] Nick Stinnett, "In Search of Strong Families," in *Building Family Strengths: Blueprints for Action*, ed. Nick Stinnett, Barbara Chesser and John DeFrain (Lincoln, Nebraska: The University of Nebraska Press, 1979), pp. 23–30.

[21] Paul C. Rosenblatt and Roxanne M. Anderson, "Interaction in Farm Families: Tension and Stress," in *The Family in Rural Society*, ed. Coward and Smith, pp. 147–166.

[22] Smith and Coward, "The Family in Rural Society: Images of the Future," p. 221.

[23] Coward, "Demythologizing the Farm Family," p. 20.

[24] Brown, "A Quarter Century of Trends."

[25] David L. Brown and J. M. O'Leary, *Labor Force Activity in Metropolitan and Nonmetropolitan America* (Washington, D.C.: U.S. Department of Agriculture, 1979); L. Chenoweth and E. Maret-Havens, "Women's Labor Force Participation: A Look at Some Residential Patterns," *Monthly Labor Review*, 101 (1978), 38–41.

[26] Linda A. Bescher-Donnelly and Leslie Whitner Smith, "The Changing Roles and Status of Rural Women," in *The Family in Rural Society*, ed. Coward and Smith, pp. 167–185.

[27] Coward and Smith, "Families in Rural Society."

[28] Coward, "Demythologizing the Farm Family."

[29] Jonathan P. Sher, ed., *Education in Rural America: A Reassessment of Conventional Wisdom* (Boulder, Colorado: Westview Press, 1977).

[30] Victor A. Christopherson, Barry R. Bainton and Monica C. Escher, *Alcohol Usage Patterns Among the Rural Aged in Arizona* (Tucson, Arizona: Office of Human Development and Family Research, University of Arizona, 1980).

[31] Raymond T. Coward and Richard K. Kerckhoff, *The Rural Elderly: Program Planning Guidelines* (Ames, Iowa: North Central Regional Center for Rural Development, 1978); William R. Lassey, Marie L. Lassey, Gary R. Lee and Naomi Lee, eds., *Research and Public Policy with the Rural Elderly* (Corvallis Oregon: Western Rural Development Center, 1980); Dennis A. Watkins and Charles O. Crawford, eds., *Rural Gerontology Research in the Northeast* (Ithaca, New York: Northeast Regional Center for Rural Development, 1977).

[32] James W. Flax, Morton O. Wagenfeld, Ruby E. Ivens and Robert J. Weiss, *Mental Health and Rural America: An Overview and Annotated Bibliography*, DHEW Publication No. (ADM) 78-753 (Washington, D.C.: U.S. Government Printing Office, 1979).

[33] Philip Taietz and Sande Milton, "Rural-Urban Differences in the Structure of Services for the Elderly in Upstate New York Counties," *Journal of Gerontology*, 34, no. 3 (1979), 429–437.

[34] Toby Cedar and John Salasin, *Research Directions for Rural Mental Health* (McLean, Virginia: MITRE Corporation, 1979); Gary Nelson, "Social Services to the Urban and Rural Aged: The Experience of Area Agencies on Aging," *The Gerontologist*, 20, no. 2 (1980), 200–207.

[35] Raymond T. Coward, Richard K. Kerckhoff and Robert W. Jackson, "Rural Family Development: A Delivery System for Social Programs," presented at the Fourth World Congress of Rural Sociology, Torun, Poland, August 1976 (ERIC-CRESS 144755); Leon H. Ginsberg, *Social Work in Rural Communities: A Book of Readings* (New York: Council on

Social Work Education, 1976); Philip Taietz, "Community Facilities and Social Services," in *Rural Environments and Aging*, ed. R. C. Atchley and T. O. Byerts (Washington, D.C.: The Gerontological Society, 1975), pp. 145–156; Anne S. Williams, "Planning Service Delivery Systems for Rural, Sparsely Populated Areas," in *Aspects of Planning for Public Services in Rural Areas*, ed. David L. Rogers and Larry R. Whiting (Ames, Iowa: North Central Regional Center for Rural Development, 1976), pp. 202–234.

³⁶ Peter A. Keller and J. Dennis Murray, eds., *Handbook of Rural Community Mental Health* (New York: Human Sciences Press, 1982); Morton O. Wagenfeld, ed., *Perspectives on Rural Mental Health* (San Francisco: Jossey-Bass Inc., Publishers, 1981); Raymond T. Coward and William M. Smith, eds., *Family Services: Issues and Opportunities in Contemporary Rural America* (Lincoln, Nebraska: The University of Nebraska Press, 1983).

³⁷ Coward and Smith, "Families in Rural Society."

³⁸ USDA, *A Time to Choose*, p. 34.

³⁹ USDA, *A Time to Choose*, p. 31.

⁴⁰ Eugene A. Wilkening, "Farm Families and Family Farming," in *The Family in Rural Society*, ed. Coward and Smith, pp. 27–37.

⁴¹ USDA, *A Time to Choose*, p. 31.

⁴² Joseph Davenport III and Judith A. Davenport, "Regional and State Institutes: Rx for Human Services in Boomtowns," in *Social Work in Rural Areas: Issues and Opportunities*, ed. Joseph Davenport III, Judith A. Davenport and James R. Wiebler (Laramie, Wyoming: Office of Conferences and Institutes, University of Wyoming, 1980), pp. 34–47.

⁴³ Raymond T. Coward, "Rural Families Changing But Retain Distinctiveness," *Rural Development Perspectives*, 3 (1980), 7.

⁴⁴ Raymond T. Coward, "Planning Community Services for the Rural Elderly: Implications from Research," *The Gerontologist*, 19, no. 3 (1979), 275–282.

⁴⁵ Gary R. Lee and Marie L. Lassey, "Rural-Urban Residence and Aging: Directions for Future Research," in *Research and Public Policy with the Rural Elderly*, ed. Lassey, Lassey, Lee and Lee, pp. 77–88.

⁴⁶ J. L. Shover, *First Majority—Last Minority: The Transforming of Rural Life in America* (DeKalb, Illinois: Northern Illinois University Press, 1976).

⁴⁷ Glenn R. Hawkes, Nancy G. Kutner, Miriam J. Wells, Victor A. Christopherson and Edwin B. Almirol, "Families in Cultural Islands," in *The Family in Rural Society*, ed. Coward and Smith, pp. 87–125.

⁴⁸ Hawkes, et al., "Families in Cultural Islands," p. 89.

⁴⁹ Peter L. Heller and Gustava M. Quesada, "Rural Familism: An Interregional Analysis," *Rural Sociology*, 42 (1977), 220–240; Peter A. Heller, Gustava M. Quesada, David L. Harvey and Lyle G. Warner, "Rural Familism: Interregional Analysis," in *The Family in Rural Society*, ed. Coward and Smith, pp. 73–85; Peter A. Heller, Gustava M. Quesada, David L. Harvey and Lyle G. Warner, "Familism in Rural and Urban America: A Critique and Reconceptualization of a Construct," *Rural Sociology*, 46 (1981), in press.

⁵⁰ Donn A. Derr, Nelson L. LeRay and Charles O. Crawford, "Delineating Rural Development Policy," *Human Services in the Rural Environment*, 1, no. 6 (1980), 3–8.

⁵¹ Derr, LeRay and Crawford, "Delineating Rural Development Policy," p. 8.

⁵² Larry Farmer, Mississippi Action for Community Education, comments at the second Chautauqua in Mississippi, "Change and Tradition in the American Small Town," sponsored by the Center for Small Town Research and Design, Mississippi State University, April 9, 1981.

⁵³ U.S. Department of Commerce, Bureau of the Census, "Social and Economic Characteristics of the Metropolitan and Nonmetropolitan Population: 1977 and 1970," *Current Population Reports; Special Studies, p. 25, No. 75* (Washington, D.C.: U.S. Government Printing Office, November 1978).

⁵⁴ Elo, "The Changing Rural Economy," pp. 1–8.

⁵⁵ Smith and Coward, "Images of the Future," pp. 229.

An Overview of Rural
Economic Development Policy

DAVID SZCZERBACKI

Introduction

Economic development policy as the phrase is used here, includes two activities supported by federal/state funding: planning and investment of public resources to stimulate local or substate/regional economies through a variety of incentives and tools. In sketching an overview of rural economic development policy, three topics appear particularly relevant: environmental characteristics which condition policy formulation; illustrative program initiatives; and critical issues raised by the Reagan Administration's budgetcutting proposals.

I. Environmental Characterics

To discuss *rural* economic development is to recognize that, though there are similarities (e.g., effects of inflation), rural problems and policies differ in some fashion from those which are distinctively urban, metropolitan, suburban, etc. The term "rural" refers to, among others, the following environmental characteristics:[1]

A. *Demography*. The areas considered here are non-Standard Metropolitan Statistical Areas (SMSA) characterized by the existence of a few major population nodes (or "growth centers") and numerous decentralized nodes serving what is often an agricultural hinterland.[2] Some of these are experiencing (or anticipating) "boom town" phenomena—for example those with potential energy resources. In many other rural areas, however, young persons are leaving and there are the corresponding problems associated with an "aging" population.

B. *Economy*. Rural economies tend to be based on exploitation of natural resources. Typically rural economies lack diversification; are highly vulnerable to shortages (e.g. energy, raw materials), the appearance of new technologies, recessionary forces, and environmental restrictions; and tend to generate incomes that are spent elsewhere because of the relative inability of such incomes to be "absorbed" by the local economy. Following the lead of the economy of the U.S. as a whole, rural economies have seen an increase in the size of the service sector. Issues that are critical in the economic development of many rural areas include the availability of the infrastructure needed to support expansion, maintenance of the quality and character of the rural environment and life-style, and the economic and social needs of those communities which are losing (or have lost) viability as "central places."

Four characteristics of rural economies warrant special attention. First, a virtual halt in unsubsidized housing construction in much of rural America—this at a time of low vacancy rates for both rental and owner-occupied units—has often made it impossible for new families to find adequate housing at a price they can afford. At the same time, elderly persons occupy "large" units which exceed both their needs and the means available to maintain such units.

Second, rural America is home to a high rate of low- and moderate-income people—particularly the elderly and minorities. Approximately 40% of the nation's poor reside in rural America. Approximately 38% of all rural blacks and 40% of all rural Indians live below the poverty level.[3] Nationwide figures show, in fact, that the incidence of sub-standard housing is three times as high in rural areas when compared to urban areas.[4]

Third, the decline in the vitality of traditional central business districts (CBD's) is a problem found in areas undergoing growth as well as in declining/stagnant areas. Typical problems include decline in commerce (particularly retail trade), vacant upper floors in commercial structures, and physical/aesthetic deterioration (e.g. dilapidated structures, false fronts, a hodge-podge of signs). CBD decline is often associated with commercial "strip development" occurring on the "outskirts of town."

Fourth, rural firms tend to encounter difficulties in gaining access to capital markets[5] as a result either of failure to attract outside capital *into* an area or of the *outward flow* of indigenous capital to more lucrative investment opportunities.

C. *Government Institutions.* The character of rural government is, in large part, a reflection of "home rule" powers granted to local governments by individual state legislatures. Many rural jurisdictions continue to maintain "Commission" and/or "Weak Executive" forms of local government which serve to foster parochialism and contribute to a leadership void. Often rural governments are also characterized by a fragmentation and overlapping of effort in providing services. Many rural towns, townships, villages, boroughs, parishes, "small cities," etc., lack the "expertise" (e.g., management, grantsmanship) that is so often required in administering and/or acquiring federal and state program dollars. These towns typically lack the fiscal resources needed to underwrite and/or promote economic development, yet their political leadership, on balance, tends to be wary of state and federal government programs in general, and, in particular of those programs that must be supported, in the long run, by local dollars. The problems of rural governments have been summarized thus:

> Whether small community needs are those associated with growth or decline, they pose special problems for local governments. . . . Given their small population bases, small rural governments are limited in the array of public services they can provide . . . while the range of public services offered by rural governments is more limited (compared to urban areas), the per unit costs of providing these services is usually higher. . . .
>
> Many small towns, remote from Washington and from their state capitals, lack the "grantsmanship" that is so often required to compete successfully for limited Federal and state assistance. This difficulty is compounded by the fact that many federal programs have been formulated with big cities in mind. As a result, such programs frequently contain eligibility and other criteria that hinder access by small communities. Even when assistance is available, the lack of fiscal resources makes it difficult for many small communities to match federal grants and to repay loans.[6]

D. *Values*—The idea that self-reliance, initiative and independence are characteristics of rural residents is part of American folklore. While there is evidence that both urban and rural America are evolving toward a "mass society,"[7] information compiled by the "Gallup Opinion Index" between June 1965 and April 1975 indicates considerable differences in the values of urban and rural residents.[8] More specifically, research completed by Campbell, Converse and Rogers in compiling a nationwide composite "Index of Well-Being" found that rural residents tend to have a greater sense of "well-being" than their urban counterparts,[9] a characteristic which may help to explain two others—resistance to change and a corresponding faith in the integrity and permanence of social institutions—which seem prevalent among rural Americans.[10] Finally, a tradition of "self-help" among rural residents in confronting common problems can be traced to the earliest days of the American culture. This tradition has been institutionalized in the structure of the U.S. Department of Agriculture Cooperative Extension Service, in land-grant colleges, and in cooperatives funded by the Office of Economic Opportunity.[11]

II. Illustrative Program Initiatives

There has long been considerable interest on the national political level in shaping or addressing rural problems. Historically this interest has been one of promoting agricultural interests—as evidenced, for example, in legislation passed as early as 1789 establishing a "land policy of dispersed ownership."[13] Interest in promoting broader economic-development interests dates back to the passage of the Areawide Development Act of 1961, the Appalachian Development Act of 1962, the Public Works and Economic Development Act of 1965, and the Rural Development Act of 1972. More recently, on September 24, 1980, President Carter signed into law the Small Community and Rural Development Policy Act (P.L. 99-259). As one of its numerous proposals, this policy statement called for the coordination of rural development programs at the federal level—including the development of a comprehensive rural development strategy by the U.S. Department of Agriculture.

In addition to programs designed specifically for rural America, it is interesting to note, urban-oriented programs and agencies have a stake in rural economic development concerns. The Department of Housing and *Urban* Development, for example, offers two popular economic-development programs which find rural communities and firms competing against their metropolitan/urban counterparts: the Urban Development Action Grant program and the Community Development Block Grant/Small Cities program.

Presently, approximately 714 individual federal programs are available to aid a broad range of rural development efforts, including fifty different functional categories (e.g., accelerating rural industrial and business growth, small business, general housing, etc.) and five general categories (including Jobs, Business, Industry; Community Facilities; Community Functions and Services; Housing; and Planning and Coordination). These 714 programs range from such diverse activities as efforts to accelerate business growth to programs supporting library facilities and museums.[14]

Federal spending for rural economic development has been concentrated in four key areas:

A. Targeted Economic Development—targeted according to severity of need for the development of business/industry particularly through the development of community facilities.

B. Public and Private Infrastructure—typically including an addition to a community's capital stock—housing, transportation, communications; similar to targeted economic development.

C. Human Capital—includes a variety of education, health, manpower, and training programs; the federal government has had less discretion in expenditure of these funds than it has in targeted economic development and public and private infrastructure programs; involved with human services as opposed to physical development; approximately 60% of these dollars are spent in the area of education.

D. Transfer Payments—assistance targeted to persons not locations; federal government has limited discretion over expenditure of these funds; largest categories of assistance include social security retirement and disability.[15]

In addition to such federal initiatives, state and local governments offer a range of programs in support of rural economic development. Such programs range from corporate income-tax exemption to state financing of speculative building construction.[16] States vary as to the economic-development incentives they offer. One of the more popular tools is, and has been, the tax-exempt industrial revenue bond, first authorized in Mississippi in 1936. State-sponsored and/or -authorized Industrial Development Agencies (authorized to issue such bonds) currently exist in some thirty-two states.[17] States also differ with respect to conditions *not* favorable to economic development (e.g. progressive state income-tax structure, unduly burdensome environmental regulations). One result of such interstate differences has been a phenomenon of interstate competition whereby states seek to influence a migration of capital (and people) from other states to their own.[18]

As one might expect, the existence of such a vast array of program alternatives has contributed to monumental coordination problems throughout, between, and among program delivery systems. The multiplicity of rural development initiatives has created a condition described as follows:

> . . . the image of federal grant assistance application requirements, eligibility standards, audits and deadlines that have burdened small town and rural officials has made it nearly impossible to address rural problems effectively.[19]
>
> . . . it is apparent the micropolitan (nonmetropolitan) areas have no federal policy at all, only a confused set of piecemeal programs administered by disjointed federal fiefdoms jealous of their narrow self-interests and unable to view micropolitan areas as needing an integrated, systematic policy that is economically efficient and equitable.[20]

Given the state of rural economic development policy, a legitimate research question would include the identification of the manner in which expert analysts might contribute to the resolution of the coordination problem. In addition, one might explore the extent to which expert analysts contribute to this problem.

More broadly, the "coordination problem" related to rural development program delivery systems raises fundamental structural questions regarding the concept of "fiscal federalism." Are the eligibility and performance requirements attached to federal grants-in-aid worth the bother for local officials? Is the nation's "best interest" served by "block-grant" programs which emphasize local discretion in the expenditure of federal dollars? What are the most appropriate roles for state governments in programs that link federal largesse to both sub-state units of government and the private sector? What roles are most appropriately filled by interstate and sub-state regional organizations (e.g. Federal Regional Councils in the former case, sub-state Regional Clearinghouses in the latter case)?

As we enter a period which is likely to see *at least* a leveling-off in federal funding for rural development programs, policy emphasis will focus as much on the way programs are "delivered" as it will on the substantive nature of such programs. The rhetoric of national policy statements notwithstanding, efforts to develop and

implement programs related to "community development" strategies for small rural towns have not, typically, done justice to the
task at hand. Too often there is a gap between policy objectives and
performance.

The reasons for such a shortfall include (but certainly are not
limited to) the fact that community development efforts in (and/or
for) small towns tend to be fragmented, "shot-in-the-dark" en-
deavors. Comprehensiveness, a catch-phrase of most federal and
state community-development grant, loan, and planning programs, is rarely evident in the implementation of community-
development programs. Little attention is paid to the process of
community-development planning and implementation in small
towns. What, for example, are the essential ingredients for successful "program development" or "grantsmanship" efforts in the
typical rural "central places?"

III. Issue Agenda: Limits to Government Intervention

Government intervention in rural (and urban) economic decisionmaking processes (e.g., affecting the nature and location of investments) raises fundamental questions about the role of government
in "picking winners" from the ebb-and-flow process of economic
growth and decline. This role is being seriously questioned as
national and state policymakers react to the Reagan Administration's proposals to reduce drastically the portfolio of programs supporting rural (and urban) economic development programs. In a
very important sense, such debate is a "watershed" opportunity for
assessing the appropriateness of government economic intervention.

As government expands its role in developing and implementing
targeted investment strategies for regions, counties, cities, or "en-
terprise zones," changes can be effected in the very nature of our
economic system.[21] Government intervention, predicated on the
assumption that economic security and stability are paramount,
can be seen as being contrary to the underlying value structure of
the free-enterprise system. Lester Thurow, among others, has
noted the roots of this value conflict:

> The growth of large economic institutions . . . forces government to
> take many protective actions. At the heart of capitalism and competi-

tive market lies the doctrine of failure. The inefficient are to be driven out of business by the efficient. But governments cannot tolerate the failure of large economic actors. . . .

But if we rescue large economic actors, this creates a demand for rescuing the local grocery store or the small town from its mistakes. Unless we do so, we have a double standard for the large and the small when it comes to failure. But to rescue is to control. It is also to undercut the whole doctrine of competitive capitalism. Those who fail won't be punished economically.[22]

Government actions taken to target investment activities have at least three consequences—described in the *1981 Economic Report of the President* as part of a discussion of the "Dilemma of Industrial Policy."

First, a successful policy of identifying and supporting promising sectors implies a willingness on the part of the government to let some of the firms in the chosen sectors fail. . . . However, the government's necessary sensitivity to income losses, intensified by the fact that it would bear a special responsibility for a chosen sector, makes it difficult, if not impossible to tolerate such a portfolio. The more likely outcome . . . would be a reluctance to abandon individual firms that fail. This could more than offset any gains achieved by the successful few among the chosen firms.

Second, there could be a tendency to implement a strategy of picking winners by excessive reliance upon policies where the government has broader discretion (e.g. trade policies) rather than designing policies specific to the problem at hand. The resulting use of easily available, but not necessarily efficient, policy instruments would create an unbalanced response and introduce additional distortions and rigidities into the economy. Adding to this tendency would be the policymakers' inevitable recognition that a policy tool designed for one purpose can often be used for another.

Third, to avoid "wasteful duplication" the government would be likely to centralize the process of picking winners. Such centralization would forgo the advantages of risk-diversification that come from decentralized decisionmaking and would further heighten the pressures to protect losers among the chosen sectors.[23]

Clearly, intervention into the free-market economy can be rationalized on the basis of efficiency and/or equity criteria. However, a "Dilemma of Industrial Policy" exists since such intervention "carries with it both the potential to improve and the threat of reducing the economy's efficiency and adaptability."[24]

Where an industrial policy of "picking winners" *is* implemented,
it seems imperative that efforts to reduce the opportunity for market distortions be made explicit. One means toward this end is to
insulate from political meddling—national, state, or local—
economic development programs financed by the public sector.
Decisions on the awarding of grants, loans, and loan guarantees,
for example, can be left to those experts skilled in the art and
science of "picking winners." Indeed, such insulation is at least
formally structured into most, if not all, public-sector programs.

Where such insulation does occur in fact—and to the extent that
it occurs—possibilities for market distortion remain. Information
pertinent to private-sector investment decisions needs to be
brought to the attention of these decision-makers. At first glance,
this assertion might be challenged by advocates of a free-market
economy—one devoid of government intervention. Such advocates argue that economic rewards should accrue to "opportunity
seekers."[25]

One problem, of course, with this argument is that differences
exist among existing and prospective entrepreneurs regarding the
distribution of "capacities" necessary to seek such opportunities.
One suspects, for example, that many areas of the rural South are
not sharing in the much publicized "Sunbelt" growth phenomenon
(at least partially) because they lack qualified decision-makers.

It is important to note that entrepreneurship implies a basic set
of capabilities—as, for example, defined by Leibenstein:

> The entrepreneur must: (a) have the ability to discover investment
> opportunities, and/or (b) the ability to seek information the analysis of
> which can lead to the discovery of investment opportunities. . . .
> . . . related growth-contributing activities are the ferreting out of
> new investment opportunities, the invention of new production proc-
> esses or techniques, the discovery of new resources and commodities,
> the teaching and learnings of skills, the spreading of ideas, and, finally,
> the important act of savings . . .[26]

A second problem related to the phenomenon of "opportunity-
seeking" involves what Clark terms the "availability of information
and its implications":

> Formidable problems exist with respect to the basic flow of data. Infor-
> mation concerning national changes, and the concomitant regional

changes that are called for, must somehow reach local decision makers. The extent of this information flow, in both qualitative and quantitative terms, is an important consideration to regional growth and development. This question may continue to be a problem in geographically isolated regions despite modern communications technology.

The media are ubiquitous but even so it cannot be denied that information flows vary from region to region. If a local enterpreneur is to fulfill his initiative role he must have the information available and furthermore it must be sufficiently detailed and precise that he can see accurately and rapidly what the implications are for his activities.[27]

To the extent that entrepreneurial capacities and resources are limited in rural areas, the problems and imperatives identified by Leibenstein and Clark are relevant. It seems relatively safe to assume that various economic development experts have significant roles to play in communicating investment-related information to prospective enterpreneurs. Likewise, it seems quite valid to hypothesize that failure to implement public-sector economic development programs is due, at least in part, to barriers to such communication processes.

Concern with questions relating to both the delivery structure and the scope of rural economic development programs is part of a larger debate regarding the appropriateness of government intervention in the private economy. If a case can be made that rural economies suffer from both communication deficiencies and related capital-market distortions (as they appear to), rural economy development policy can be "rationalized" in a fashion that pays due respect to conservative economic criteria of appropriateness (such as those raised by the Reagan Administration) while satisfying such deficiencies and distortions. Such an approach to policy formulation is preferable, one would think, to a "meat-axe" approach calling for wholesale dismantling of rural economic development programs.

NOTES

[1] For an overview of "contemporary rural America" see: Thomas R. Ford, *Rural U.S.A. Persistence and Change* (ed.), Ames, Iowa: Iowa State University Press, 1978; Also, Dennis L. Little, "Changing Demographic Patterns and Some Potential Implications for

Rural America," Washington: National Educational Institute For Economic Development, 1980.

²Kenneth D. Rainey and Karen D. Rainey, "Rural Government and Local Public Services, in Ford, Chapter 8. Authors note that "Thirty percent of the U.S. population lived outside the Standard Metropolitan Areas in 1970. Eight percent (16 million) lived in nonmetropolitan municipalities of less than 10,000 people, while another 15 percent (31 million) lived in unincorporated parts of non-metropolitan areas. . . . at least 1 American in 4 lives in a small, rural local government jurisdiction."

³The Carter Administration, *Small Community and Rural Development Policy*, Washington: The White House, 12/20/79, p. 3.

⁴Kenneth L. Deavers and David L. Brown, *Social and Economic Trends in Rural America*, Washington: United States Department of Agriculture, October 1979, p. 1.

⁵Council for Northeast Economic Action, *Public Financing Issues—An Analysis of Gaps in the Capital Market* (Number Two In a Series), Boston, Mass.: An Analysis Prepared for the Appalachian Regional Commission, 1980.

⁶The Carter Administration (1979), p. 4.

⁷Olaf F. Larson and Everett M. Rogers, "Rural Society in Transition: The American Setting," in James H. Copp, ed., *Our Changing Rural Society: Perspectives and Trends*, Ames, Iowa: Iowa State University Press, 1964.

⁸For an analysis of the data compiled in the "Gallup Opinion Index," see: Olaf F. Larson, "Values and Beliefs of Rural People," in Ford, Chapter 6.

⁹Angus Campbell, Philip E. Converse, and William L. Rodgers, *The Quality of American Life: Perceptions, Evaluations and Satisfactions*, New York: Russell Sage, 1976, pp. 51, 234–238.

¹⁰Claude S. Fischer considers the cause of such resistance to be a lack of a "critical mass" of normative support for change in rural areas—A support that does characterize urban environments: "The Effect of Urban Life on Traditional Values," *Social Forces* 53 (March 1975), 421; Also, recent research indicates that "persons who live in rural areas are more likely to favor de-emphasizing growth than persons who live in cities and suburbs." See: Jon Czarnecki, Harry Klodowski, Lester Milbrath, "Beliefs About Economic Growth," *Growth and Change*, October 1980, pp. 36–41.

¹¹Brian M. Phifer, E. Frederick List, and Boyd Faulkner, "History of Community Development in America," in James A. Christenson and Jerry W. Robinson, Jr., eds., *Community Development In America*, Ames, Iowa: Iowa State University Press, 1980, Chapter 2; Also, Sar A. Levithan, *The Great Society's Poor Law—A New Approach to Poverty*, Baltimore: The John Hopkins Press, 1969, Chapter 10.

¹³W. Neill Schaller, "Public Policy and Rural Social Change," in Ford, pp. 199–210.

¹⁴U.S. Dept. of Agriculture, *Guide to Federal Program for Rural Development*, Washington: USDA Rural Development Service, March 1975.

¹⁵Deavers and Brown, p. 29.

¹⁶14th Annual Report, "The Fifty Legislative Climates . . . ," *Industrial Development*, January/February 1980, pp. 2–15.

¹⁷Andrew J. Aulde, *The Effectiveness of State and Local Industrial Development Incentive Mechanisms*, Ithaca, N.Y.: Cornell University Program in Urban and Regional Studies, Occasional Paper #10, August 1980, p. 42. It should be noted that Industrial Revenue Bonds (IRB's) have come under attack in some states due to alleged "abuses" relating to the financing of "non-industrial" commercial projects. Concern also exists with the loss of public revenue resulting from IRB "tax exempt" or "payment in lieu of tax" provisions.

¹⁸"The Second War Between the States," *Business Week*, May 17, 1976.

¹⁹U.S. Dept. of Agriculture, *Rural Development Progress, June 1977–June 1979, Fifth Report of the Secretary of Agriculture to Congress*, Washington: USDA, October 1979, p. 23.

²⁰Luther L. Tweeten and George L. Brinkman, *Micropolitan Development*, Ames: Iowa State Univ. Press, 1976, p. 423.

[24] See, for example, Mark B. Urben, "Using Locally Planned Investment Strategies For Strategic Targetting of EDA Investment Funds," Economic Development Research Report prepared for the Office of Economic Research, Economic Development Administration, U.S. Department of Commerce, November 30, 1977.

[22] Lester C. Thurow, *The Zero-Sum Society*, New York: Basic Books, 1980, pp. 21–22.

[23] Council of Economic Advisers, *Economic Report of the President*, Washington: U.S. Government Printing Office, 1981, pp. 127–130.

[24] Ibid., p. 127.

[25] Peter D. C. Clark, *Attitudes and Behavior: Underlying Factors in Regional Opportunity Loss*, Ithaca, N.Y.: Cornell Dissertations in Planning, Cornell University, June 1974, p. 109.

[26] Harvey Leibenstein, *Economic Backwardness and Economic Growth*, New York: Wiley, 1957, pp. 120, 121.

[27] Clark, p. 109.

The Role of
Environmental Psychology
in Small Town Planning and Research

JAMES C. BROWN

Psychologists, sociologists, and town planners have long been concerned with the relationship between the physical structure of a community and the values, attitudes, and behavior of its citizens. On one hand, physical-ecological determinists stress the importance of physical variables such as architecture, size of the community, and heterogeneity of the residents as major determinants of values, attitudes, and behavior; social psychologists, on the other hand, emphasize the role of more subjective elements such as perceptions, cognitions, and evaluations. An important subfield of behavioral science, environmental psychology, bridges the theoretical and empirical gap between these objective and subjective approaches. That is, environmental psychology concerns itself with the interrelation between man's environment and his perception of that environment. To illustrate this point please consider the following scene: *A boy enters a curb-side market and buys a soft drink. He opens the can and drinks the contents. There is no trash container in sight so he throws the can on the ground and leaves.*

On the surface, the focus here would appear to be on an insignificant bit of human action. Note, however, that the boy is only one of the players in this scene; there is another equally important actor, the environment. By virtue of what it is, what is located in it, and what is not located in it, the environment made the boy's actions possible. Had the setting been a school yard rather than the town street he would not have decided to have the soft drink. Had there been houses located here rather than the store, he would not have bought the drink. Had there been a trash can available he might not have littered. In other words, the envi-

99

ronment influenced the boy's behavior. And by leaving the soft drink can on the ground he altered his surroundings. He changed the world that would be encountered by the next person who came behind him. What is represented here is not just action but interaction—the interaction between man and his environment. Such interaction is the subject of environmental psychology, a field of concern to anyone involved with the small town, its planning, and its development.

Most people are conditioned to see themselves as something apart from the world around them. Their environment is something that they can manipulate and change according to their own needs. If they want a town where trees and fields are now, they cut down trees, pave fields, and build buildings. If they then decide that they want the trees and fields, they tear the buildings down, break up the concrete, plant trees and call it a park. They are forever altering the world around them. Most of them, however, are not cognizant of the fact that the world is also manipulating them, that they behave a certain way in the fields and woods, another way in school, and yet another way in the park. Whatever the nature of their environment, it has a significant impact on their behavior. Psychologists have even suggested that people do not just learn ways of behaving per se but rather ways associated with particular times and places. Throughout their lives, what they think, what they feel, what they do is really an interaction with the environment and cannot be separated from it. Even their arrival in this world may have been stimulated by the romantic setting where their parents happened to be nine months before they were born. And on a slightly more negative note their leaving this world will probably be helped along by environmental factors as well: polluted air and water, inadequate housing, or even a speeding car ignoring a stop sign.

However, even though the influence of the environment on behavior is significant, I am not suggesting that there is a direct cause-and-effect relationship. Rather, the form of the perception of the environment provides an essential mediating effect. There is an old line that goes, "I know you think you understood what I said but what you thought you heard is not what I meant." Similarly, what people see is not necessarily what is there. Reality tends to be individual and subjective. The effect of the environment, then, is actually a function of two separate elements as well as the two elements in interaction. The first of these is the environment itself—those things that do exist in our world. The second is the personal, perceptual filter made up of previous learning experiences, individual needs, tastes, and values. For example, to a person raised in Mize, Mississippi, Jackson may seem a fast-paced, crowded, frightening city. To a native of Chicago or New York, on the other hand, Jackson will seem mild and slow by comparison. Two significant aspects of this subjective perception of the environment are selective attention and habituation.

Of the array of stimuli in their environment people pay attention to only a selected number; they attend to what they want or need to perceive and screen out the rest, the selection being determined by two factors. First, they tend to focus on those things that they perceive as relevant to their needs, and to exclude things that they see as irrelevant to them. For example, a driver of a car is more likely to be attuned to landmarks and to recall directions than is a passenger in the car. In another vein, what features of an attractive woman will be the object of focus depends upon whether the viewer is male or female: the female will be likely to attend primarily to clothes, jewelry, make-up and hairdo, while initially the male will tend to perceive her "natural endowments".

Besides one's perception of relevance, expectations help to determine selective attention to the environment. As a general rule of thumb, people are most likely to attend to information that is consistent with their pre-established impressions and expectation. Environmental perception operates on the same principle. I have friends who love to visit New Orleans, for example, and come away talking about the fun, excitement and glitter of the French Quarter. I have other friends who despise New Orleans and report on the dirty streets, the strange and perverted inhabitants and the watered-down drinks in the French Quarter: a single environment but two different expectations and therefore two different perceptions.

The second factor that serves to distort perception of the environment is habituation, that is, the human tendency to become less and less aware and consequently less responsive to aspects of the environment after one has become accustomed to it. The sights and sounds of a hospital setting, for example, tend to evoke a very negative reaction for most patients and visitors. On the other hand, nurses, physicians, and other hospital staff members come to take their environment for granted. Some people have had the experience of moving into a new house where some of the rooms are painted a color that is particularly unattractive to them. If for some reason they cannot immediately repaint the room it gradually will come to seem less unattractive and they may even stop thinking about repainting.

Of all the elements relating to our perception of the environment, habituation is one of the most significant concerns to those who are directly involved in altering the environment and people's attitudes toward that environment. This is so because habituation brings toleration, oftentimes even without awareness, of unacceptable environmental conditions. Residents of Los Angeles and Birmingham will have a more favorable perception of the quality of the air in those cities than will visitors. By the same token, residents in certain areas become habituated to jet-flight patterns directly over their bedrooms, to having to drive fifty miles to find adequate shopping facilities or to having lakes and rivers polluted. The point is that all of those involved in small-town planning, research, and design have an ethical responsibility to be aware of issues such as habituation and to realize that the absence of a demand for an improved environment can be a matter of habituation, not of lack of concern.

The fact that people can become habituated to environmental conditions does not mean, however, that those environmental conditions cease to affect behavior. Small-town residents, for example, may get accustomed to having no restaurants or to limited shopping and recreation facilities, but a business or industry considering locating in that town may decide not to come on the basis of the lack of such facilities.

To emphasize an important point again, a simple, one-to-one causal relationship simply does not exist between physical or environmental factors and the behavior of the people in those environments. Consequently, the town planner and designer cannot assume automatically that the town's residents will react favorably to proposed renovations of the buildings on Main Street. Subjective perceptions must also be taken into account. Here environmental and social psychologists can play an essential role because of their concern with subjective perceptions ranging from those that determine the extent of use that a park gets, to those that shape patterns of social interaction in the community and attitudes about leaving, coming to and staying in the community.

My own position is that both objective and subjective data are valuable in the planning of any change in the environment of a small town. For example, a central YMCA facility is seeking to determine the reason for a significant lack of financial support for satellite recreation facilities in small communities which seemingly would have the same need for such facilities as larger ones. Objectively, one can cite statistics as to the number of residents in each community who would seem to be more likely to utilize "Y" facilities, as to the economic base of each community, and as to the number and quality of available facilities. Subjectively, however, studies show that permanent residents fail to perceive a need for these facilities, that they do not perceive the facilities to be important to their lifestyle, and that they perceive similar facilities in a larger metropolitan area twenty to thirty miles away to be conveniently available. Here, objective data point to demand and need for recreation facilities but the subjective data point in the opposite direction. Both types of information must be considered. Either an attempt to change attitudes and perceptions without carefully looking into their sources in the objective environment or a decision to go ahead and locate the facilities in the community without knowing whether the residents will notice or care will be less than totally effective. In fact—and here is the key point—objective and subjective perceptions *together* determine the extent to which residents will use the recreational facilities; what the current residents do will in turn affect future perceptions and future decisions about additional facilities.

In conclusion, then, I would encourage those who are in any way involved in environmental changes in small towns to seek out and take advantage of both subjective and objective data. Social scientists can help here by exploring the perceptions of citizens and the kind of behavior these perceptions result in, and by examining the objective characteristics that might influence perceptions and behavior.

Concerning Small Towns:

Notes on Semiotic Process

DAN HAYS

Small towns and rural areas are made up of physical forms, some constructed by human beings and others generated by natural processes of geology, plant physiology, and so on. Most human concern lies in the realm of meanings and implications of these forms which extend beyond their description as bare physical structures. Within the settings of small towns and rural areas, human beings (and other creatures) interact with one another and the physical environment. These activities are also interpreted and may be related, often quite selectively to a notion of "small town and rural life."

Of particular interest are several aspects of *semiotic processes* as they relate to "small towns and rural areas," especially their built environment. Involved are not only the distinctive connotations of buildings, paths, and other architectural features, but also the meanings a person attributes to himself or others as residents or users of certain kinds of physical structures. Treating the built environment as a "presentational symbol," with intended reflections upon the self, is certainly an important component of many persons' relationship to physical spaces, though one not widely discussed. Important also are practical meanings associated with features of the built environment of the small town and related to possible behavior which is in some way permitted by, facilitated by, or "called for" by certain physical settings. Thus, the meanings of the small town or rural area and its component parts are highly variable, not only from one experiencer or interpreter to another but in an approximate and aggregate sense, historically.

Participants in this conference have noted a number of changes in the actual status of non-urban areas, including not only renewed economic activity and some shift vis-a-vis major technologies but also changes in the relations of inhabitants of these areas to their environments. The applied semiotician would predict that before too long there will emerge a new mythology or popular summary conceptualization of small town/rural areas which takes into account some of the features documented by scholars contributing to this volume (e.g., the changed relation to urban resources and technology) but which perhaps will also emphasize the endurance of some earlier values (e.g., individual competence, entrepreneurial initiative, wish for contact with plant and animal life, and so on). Meanwhile, and probably forever, some features of actual small towns will, for diverse persons, have meanings that may never be discussed at a conference or summarized in popular stereotypes.

I

A fundamental distinction made in semiotic studies, and in some other academic disciplines which are concerned with meanings, is between what is "meant" (in classical terms, the *signatum*) and how it is "signified" (the *signans*). Both make up the semiotic concept of *sign*, though sometimes the term "sign" is used to focus on just the *signans*, with the *signatum* implicit or in the background[1]. A three-way distinction is often employed between physical sign, referent (denotable event or object), and interpretant (roughly, conceptual or mental meaning). The latter distinction is important, since two or more persons observing or thinking about the identical object or event may come up with somewhat different interpretations; and the same physical sign, for example the verbal term "farm house," may be linked to dissimilar referents.

One of the appeals of semiotic analysis for architectural and cultural studies is generality in the kinds of signs and symbols investigated. In semiotic study, the human linguistic system in its more rational aspects, which in philosophic treatments receives such strong focus, is viewed as just one part of general sign-processing. In his *Logic*, for example, C. S. Peirce, an important figure in the development of modern semiotic theory, lists twelve kinds of signs, several not at all considered by traditional logicians[2]. John Lyons, in his work on semantics, has discussed several classifications of signs and commented on problems in terminology.[3]

For purposes of this paper, three general kinds of signs can be pointed out. First, *arbitrary signs* have no obvious similarity to their referent, but depend on convention and agreement for their meaning. Ordinary words in a language system are the most prevalent example, though non-linguistic signs can be arbitrary (e.g., a green light to signal that driving is permitted). A second class, *iconic signs*, bear some similarity to their referent, though they are often somewhat conventionalized and simplified. Iconic signs could be verbal or nonverbal. (For example, "clickety clack" is a verbal term that seems both to represent and imitate a certain nonverbal sound, at least to those who know the convention. The placement of Doric-like columns on the front porch of a residence could be one kind of iconicity in architectural usage, though the exact nature of the reference might be ambiguous.) A third broad class of signs, including *indicators, symptoms, clues,* etc., have in common reliance on processes of inference and existence of background knowledge for their adequate interpretation. (Certain speech sounds might indicate to an observer that the speaker is from rural Maine, for example. Certain marks on the ground might indicate that a plow was stored there.) Though we think of indicators as usually unintentional, if not inadvertent, it is well to point out that indicators can be selected intentionally (as when a man selects a certain hat or cap to indicate group membership).

Physical signs frequently occur together with other signs, so that having to interpret a completely isolated sign is an unusual situation. Relations among signs may be *syntactic,* when they have been selected and specially arranged according to definite principles of acceptable or desired structure. This syntactic structure may be grammatical as in the case of linguistic sentences, or constructional or pictorial for some nonverbal materials. The selection of signs and complexes of signs for special impact or consequence in a situation is called *rhetoric.* Just as a verbal message may be shaped by rhetorical concerns, nonverbal materials may be selected and presented for rhetorical ends. In the architectural realm small adjustments may be made to the environment. For example, a Victorian house being purchased already built has a basic architectural form not controllable by the buyer. Once bought, however, the house and grounds can be modified to present "messages" implicitly to the neighbors: depending on small features of decor, trim, flowers, how the house is painted, whether an attempt is being made at authentic restoration or whether a cedar deck will be added, how it is kept up, etc.

Presentational symbols are addressed to oneself as well as to others. We help structure our self-definition by our characteristic clothing, hairstyle, kind of residence or automobile, our concept of what politeness is, etc. We may present one aspect to the community (represented by our frontyard and the façade of our house), another to our close friends or to ourselves alone (represented in the more intimate spaces that we structure and inhabit), and still another as referent to ourselves as we might be (in our plans and dreams of spaces that we might inhabit). The use of presentational symbols may be ambiguous, suggestive, qualified, changing, and of course open to varying interpretations.

The extent of our involvement with signs and symbols, including self-presentational ones, may not be obvious. The semiotician views the world and the person as pervasively caught up in sign-meaning relations. Roman Jakobson, the Slavic-American semiotician, once remarked that we do not live in signs.[4] But we do live in structures which have been shaped to some extent by intended meanings, as well as uses. Our houses, then, though not telegrams or deliberate publicity, do extend a lot of information about us.

Recognizing the pervasiveness of sign-meaning relations in our environments and in ourselves I think is *the fundamental semiotic insight*. There is virtually no part of our environment that is not shaped to some extent by us. Since this shaping involves choice and selection of function, it also involves meaning. This applies as well to our workplaces as to our residences, to our fields and gardens as well as to our public gathering places. Our very bodies are shaped and decorated in arbitrary and meaningful ways, not just peripherally with clothing and hairstyles, but bodily with our very tissues: our habitual facial expression, our gait and pacing of movements, and other bodily indicators of cultural and personal style and expectation. This shaping extends to social forms. One of these distinctions is the rural-urban contrast. Presentational symbols signifying "rural" or "urban" can in some instances be identified for walk, gait, clothing—even house, road, or store.

II

Some of my students and I carried out a project to determine the kinds of inferences that some people make about others based on cues from manner, dress and kind of residence.[5] We were interested in two sides of the relation between persons and architecture: 1. What kind of architectural features in a residence might be preferred by persons of a certain dress and manner? 2. What kind of dress and manner would be expected of the people living in a residence with certain architectural features?

My student colleagues and I prepared photographic slides of the exterior of a number of residences and then asked sixty-six students in an introductory class to imagine the people who would choose to live in those residences and rate them on thirteen personal/social characteristics. For another set of slides showing different couples, we asked the respondents to fill out a questionnaire on the kind of architecture and decor they thought each couple would prefer. The student respondents were all residents of a medium-sized Southeastern city (population close to 150,000) and were heavily middle class, though somewhat mixed in age and ethnic background.

The data of this project were interesting. The distribution of responses was far from random. Some similarities in response seem to indicate inferences based upon stereotyped concepts of the preferences in architecture of certain kinds of people, and, though the features had not been deliberately included in the study, several characteristics distinguished rural/small town couples or settings from others.

The two residences which were judged likely to be located in non-urban areas were fairly "traditional" houses, both in wooded settings. No. 4 was more "rustic" in detail; No. 5 was larger and more expensive, with "status" cues such as a footbridge over a stream.

Respondents gave high ratings to the following characteristics as being those that would belong to persons choosing to live in house No. 4. (Numbers in parentheses are average scale ratings on a scale of 1 to 7, where 1 would be the high.)

—"warmth" of resident (2.08)

—"good taste" of resident (2.15)

—"considerate of others" (2.21)

—resident has "much character" (2.33)

—"down to earth" (opposite of "pretentious") (2.4)

Though the trait "down to earth" was here rated numerically a bit lower than some of the other traits, the people who would prefer residence No. 4 were rated as *most* down to earth compared to those who would prefer any other of the residences shown.

The following traits ranked high as belonging to people who would occupy residence No. 5, the prestigious non-urban home:

—"good taste of resident (1.65)—"warmth" of resident (2.22)— having "much character" (2.47)—"community oriented" (2.7)—"considerate of others" (2.78)

Before offering generalizations, it would be desirable to show more residences to more respondents, with the residences varying more comprehensively than it was possible to manage in this study. However, it does appear that positive traits of warmth, considerateness, and "character" are associated with some architectural configurations. Such houses are of course actually seen, and are part of the presentational symbol-store of many people. Of possible interest to architects is the association for this particular college-educated audience of a kind of woodsy traditionalism with judgments of "good taste," and an apparent further correlation of "taste" with signs of expense in traditional houses.

In the study relating the appearance of a couple to preference in architecture and decor, one of the couples was judged by 94% of the respondents to be from a small town or rural area. Several characteristics were inferred. The couple was thought to prefer "gently curved lines" in their decor by 43.9% of the respondents, with 33.3% guessing they would prefer "right angles". Only 19.7% felt they would prefer "strongly curved lines" and only 3% "sharp angles." (For other couples depicted, other patterns were expected, but will not be discussed here. For example, an "obviously" wealthy couple was thought to prefer "sharp angles" by over half of the respondents.) In harmony with the preference for gentle lines, the rural couple was thought to prefer "gentler shades, such as beige" by 48.5% of the respondents, but "deep, rich shades" by only 7.6%. About 22% each expected them to prefer either "bright or primary colors" or "strongly contrasting colors."

A majority, 66.7%, thought that the rural couple would like to have "many objects, things to look at" in their house, with the remaining 33.3% expecting they would like "uncluttered spaces." Over half, 59.1%, thought the rural couple would have "comfortable, 'overstuffed' furniture," 33.3% thought they would have "natural wood and wicker," 7.6% thought they would have many genuine antiques, and no respondents thought they would choose "'modern' chrome, glass, and leather" furniture.

A large majority, 78.8%, felt the couple would like their living areas "accessible and visible to the out-of-doors." The remaining 21.2% said the couple would like to be "closed off from out-of-doors." This item probably reveals the reliance of the respondents on inference from stereotypes, in this case association of rural people with outdoor activities. From the author's experience of living in a rural area in the region where the study was done, however, it would appear that, to the contrary, rural people prefer their living areas rather shielded from the out-of-doors, except perhaps in the summertime if they cannot afford air-conditioning and want a breeze. Though survey data are not available, it appears, in fact, that the more rural people work with the out-of-doors, the less likely they are to wish to have the outside directly visible from the inside. When not working, they seem to focus inward toward hearth areas, each other or the television. Picture windows incorporated into rural houses may serve as presentational symbols but are rarely constructional features meant to facilitate frequent viewing of the outdoors. Rural residents who have emigrated from the city seem more oriented to viewing the out-of-doors during leisure hours.

The attributions reported above are open to various interpretations. There seems to be a semantic similarity between the beliefs that people who prefer non-urban homes are "warm" and "considerate," and the belief that the rural couple would prefer "gentle" lines and colors in furnishings. It is by no means clear that the distinctive finding that the rural couple was thought to prefer gently curving lines or right angles to sharp angles or strongly curved lines has anything to do with widely publicized beliefs about the values and character of rural folk. The respondents in the study, however, made these attributions in a pattern that was far from random, suggesting that conceptualizations of rural preferences are more extensive and perhaps subtler than has been thought.

III

People outside small towns or rural areas may have views about life, environment, and work there which are quite different from those of the inhabitants. The nature of the residents, their activities, the architectural and natural settings may be viewed differently by residents and non-residents; and the implications drawn from the apparent "basic facts" of small town or rural events may also differ according to the orientation of the person concerned.

Understanding persistence and change in the *meanings* of various facets of small town / rural life is somewhat more complicated than understanding persistence and change in the *basic facts* of the American small town, a matter that is complex enough. A full depiction of change of meanings in non-urban settings—which will certainly not be attempted here—would require both an exposition of how meanings change, and a notion of what the meanings are. If such were to be attempted, semiotic discussion could profitably focus on the how of changes in meaning by examining such topics as (a) how people come to form conventions of shared understanding of the references of symbols;[6] (b) why there is a tendency to simplify, sharpen some details, wash out or level other details;[7] and (c) why there is a strong tendency to interpret environmental information according to "prototypes" or representations of typical instances.[8]) A listing of meanings that persist or change is apt to be so diverse as to be unmanageable. It might be possible and useful, however, to define and catalogue categories of people who participate in small-town existence and ultimately effect change. Their patterns of action, here called *technologies*, relate to their wants but may also relate both shared action and interchange with parts of the environment, and generally provide a linkage between the symbolic and the actual.

Events of ordinary living usually are particular in meaning and referent to small technologies and action plans. We tend to live day by day. Usually we reflect on major contexts only when major decisions need to be made or when major contrasts are pointed out. It is only at some distance, usually, that we invoke the large-scale simplifications that general thinking or strategy involves. In semiotic study, the Principle of Contrasts points out that our meanings, as well as the impulse to seek meaning in events, frequently depend on salient oppositions; and that the contrasts we pay attention to are those which are in some way functional to us or relate to other distinctions in our system of interpretation.[9] If no cities existed, for example, there would be no need to distinguish "small town life" or "small town economics." If there were no significant variations of urban and rural life we would not have reason to contrast them.

Present-day semiotics offers us less in the way of well-worked-out principles for understanding the detailed relations between physical structures or systems and the systems of symbolization and interpretation associated with them, their development and change. A "functional" distinction for a traditional semioticist makes a difference in a system of interpretation. Implications for action choices (here part of technologies) or consequences which are not strictly symbolic have not really been treated. It seems to me that we need to make room to consider these, and especially the implications of action choices. A natural byproduct would be revelation of the developmental path of some meanings and, ultimately, possible change in them.

Let us assume, then, that a semiotic system is not just an abstract arrangement of contrasts and categories shared by all interpreters of a given signum or complex of signs. Assume instead that it represents a *mass of reasoning potential and relevant knowledge* which can bear upon interpretation and implication and *which may differ from person to person*.

Under this assumption interesting phenomena about understandings as well as misunderstandings might be explained. For example, views of small town and rural phenomena can be thought of as differing according to a person's actual relation to major features of small-town versus urban life. But it is not just "views" which differ. Our conceptualizations and our intentions serve not just to gloss or interpret but also to shape our actions and our environments. It is not just understandings but also actualities which depend on our processing of meanings. We not only *understand* our environments; we *use* them and *change* them according to our current understandings and according to desirable states we would like to realize.

To understand some developments and changes in small towns and rural areas I find it convenient to establish broad categories of persons whose interpretation systems may differ according to their situation and whose technologies consequently may also differ one from another. Some possible categories might be the following.

The *Original Shapers* of the small town area may have decided to settle and seek livelihood in that place for various reasons. They are not likely to have regarded themselves as residing in Small Towns. They were the form-establishers who by meeting their own needs contributed to the aggregate which became the small town. The *forms* that their environment and their pattern of activities took are likely to have been determined heavily by what seemed the most easily acceptable ways of making their basic technologies work—for securing food and shelter, fashioning or raising goods for external trade, and for other matters they considered important. The *actual shape* of their environment is likely to have been determined heavily by these practical concerns. Other equally practical matters were probably also influential—perhaps regulatory requirements for town development, transportation for external communication and trade, and mass production and distribution arrangements in the larger society at the time the small town grew, among other examples.

Thus, few small towns are likely to have been developed according to a really thorough and intentional plan based on pre-existing ideology. (As a matter of fact, the fit of the new town or residence to previous town and residence patterns appears to be only partial in most cases, strongly constrained by available building techniques, styles, and practical requirements of changed physical and socio-economic environments.)

A second major class of interpreters and actors related to the small town scene are those who were brought up in the small town or rural area but who became increasingly oriented to urban areas. Of these there are two subclasses: the *Clingers*, who may have travelled to a nearby urban area for work, or engaged in other activities in the city, but maintained a home in the small town or rural area; and the *Returners*, who made the major decision to move to the city but who returned after awhile. Both Clingers and Returners have major ideological commitment to the small town and their version of the values and customs of significant persons there; but they accommodate themselves to at least the production/sales/distributional technologies of the city. Their involvement with the various rural-urban polarities may be reflected in their style of living, business techniques and architecture. The Returners especially are apt to incorporate urban stylistic motifs and artefacts into their housing. They are also apt to streamline rural production technologies, major farming activities, animal care, etc.

A third class of persons in small towns and rural areas are the *Influxers*. The Influxer was originally urban in residence and background but moved to a rural area (or, less frequently, to a small town) for one or another reason. We can expect most Influxers to have lacked the close familiarity with details of non-urban life that the Original Shapers and the Clingers and Returners acquired naturally. Probably they relied on external and perhaps literary accounts of small-town/rural realities in deciding to move—and perhaps in shaping their lives after the move.

Two main classes of Influxer may be distinguished. One is more ideologically oriented and chose to move to the non-urban area to realize certain values that were part of the city-based image of the country. This kind of Influxer may range from one seeking "small town chic" to one experimenting with new social forms backed by ideological orientation. The other kind of Influxer moved from the city for more direct, practical reasons (e.g., a tax writeoff or closeness to developing business opportunity). Both kinds of Influxer may bear some resemblance to a yet more venerable social type, the Frontiersperson, but their view of small town and rural structures and arrangements is likely to differ from that of the Original Shapers. In some cases, their actual contact with the non-urban physical and social environment may be slight, especially if they work in the city.

There are any number of shaded minor categories which might also be identified. *Restorers* might be either Influxers or well-off descendants of early settlers who wish to preserve some part of the small-town environment according to their view of its state at some time in the past. *Citybillies* might be essentially urban natives who selectively adopt rural or small-town presentational features—the suburbanite who wears bib overalls on weekends; the "urban cowboy"; the fanatic devotee of rural antiques or horses; the hard-sell executive in chrome-and-glass corporate headquarters who recommends solemnly our "small-town American values" and lifestyle. The *Rural-Urban Cosmopolites* are those for whom the distinction between country and city has never presented crucial life-choices. There have always been some people who move freely between city and country, either because of affluence or because of broad understanding.

These might be additionally subdivided according to apparently stronger urban or stronger rural leanings. There might also be categories of transplanted persons who felt they made a mistake— who stayed but became *Nostalgics;* or even *Embittereds*, etc. Any number of categories might be set up to facilitate our understanding of how people of various backgrounds and circumstances perceive small towns and rural settings. One way of assessing past and potential changes in the distribution and focus of meanings associated with these areas would be to tabulate the percentage of people in these categories in given locales. As the composition of a population changes, perhaps developments in environmental and social perception and interaction will also change. Critical here would be the orientation of the Original Shapers, Clingers, Returners, Influxers, *et al.* to major technologies (whether product-service, informational, or whatever) relevant to their motives, interests, and possibilities.

It is in this composite way that detailed changes occur in small towns and rural areas, mediated by meanings and intentions, and resulting in new aggregate significance and implications. Chances are that changes in the detail and balance of non-urban life have already occurred that are not recognized widely, changes in which people have applied old technologies to new problems, or new technologies to old needs. Discovery of these changes may be speeded by attention to some of the considerations I have mentioned.

NOTES

[1] A good introduction to semiotic concepts and terminology is Thomas A. Sebeok, "Semiotics: A Survey of the State of the Art", in *Current Trends in Linguistics*, vol. 12, *Linguistics and Adjacent Arts and Sciences*, ed Sebeok (The Hague: Mouton, 1974), Tome 1, pp. 211–264. The article is reprinted in Sebeok, *Studies in Semiotics: Contributions to the Doctrine of Signs*, Research Center for Language and Semiotic Studies (Indiana University), 1976, pp. 1–45. Umberto Eco, *A Theory of Semiotics* (Bloomington: Indiana Univ. Press, 1976) is also recommended as an introduction, one that is more comprehensive in fields of application. D. Preziosi's *The Semiotics of the Built Environment* (Bloomington: Indiana Univ. Press, 1979) is the most extensive single development of a schema for architectural semiotics; it is classificatory in emphasis.

[2] *The Collected Papers of C. S. Peirce*, ed. Charles Hartshorne and Paul Weiss (Cambridge: Harvard Univ. Press, 1931–1935), vol. 2, paragraphs 254–263.

[3] *Semantics* (Cambridge Univ. Press, 1977), vol. 1, ch. 4.

[4] Noted by Sebeok in "Problems in the Classification of Signs", in Sebeok, *Studies in Semiotics*, p. 76.

[5] Edward Palmer, Marti Sherrill and Minnie Tunstall worked on this study.

[6] The conventional nature of signs is widely discussed in semiotic theory. The discussion in Lyons, Ch. 3, reflects much of this thought. One of the more interesting discussions is by the philosopher David K. Lewis, who in *Convention* (Cambridge: Harvard Univ. Press, 1969), analyzes the development and maintenance of linguistic convention according to "games of cooperation."

[7] Cf. F. C. Bartlett, *Remembering* (Cambridge Univ. Press, 1932).

[8] Eleanor H. Rosch, "Basic objects in natural categories," *Cognitive Psychology 4*, (1973), pp. 328–350.

[9] A basic discussion of this principle is contained in Roland Barthes, *Elements of Semiology*, tr. Annette Lavers and Colin Smith (New York: Hill and Wang, 1968), pp. 71–82.

Contributors

Richard R. Adicks is an Assistant Professor in the Department of English at the University of Central Florida. He has published *Oviedo: Bibliography of a Town, Le Conte's Report on East Florida*, and *A Time to Keep: History of the First United Methodist Church of Oviedo, 1873–1973*. His articles have appeared in *Walt Whitman Review*, *The University Review*, *Tennyson Research Bulletin* and the *Humanities Association Bulletin*.

James C. Brown is Director of Educational Programs and an Associate Professor in the Department of Community and Oral Health, University of Mississippi Medical Center, School of Dentistry. His articles have appeared in *The Journal of the American Dental Association, Psychological Reports, The Journal of Consulting and Clinical Psychology*, and *The Journal of Negro Education*.

Raymond Thomas Coward is an Associate Professor in the Department of Special Education, Social Work and Social Services as well as a Research Associate Professor in the Center for Rural Studies at the University of Vermont. Profesor Coward's books include *The Family in Rural Society* and *Rural Family Services: Status and Needs*. He has also contributed to a number of journals in his field including *Anthropology and Education Quarterly, Journal of Home Economics, Contemporary Educational Psychology*, and *Journal of Educational Research*.

Michael Perry Dean teaches in the Department of English at the University of Mississippi. His research in the field of Southern Literature has been published in *The Southern Quarterly, The Journal of Mississippi History, The Explicator*, and *The Mississippi*

Quarterly. He has been a previous "Chautauqua" participant, presenting a paper entitled "Ellen Douglas's Small Towns: Fictional Anchors."

Daniel G. Hays is an Associate Professor of Psychology at the University of Alabama in Huntsville. He has been an NSF Fellow and has worked for the Rand Corporation. His articles have been published in *Psychological Reports* and *The Journal of the Acoustical Society of America*, among others.

John Brinkerhoff Jackson has long been one of America's foremost thinkers and writers in the field of landscape architecture and the Nation's environment. He has served as editor and publisher of *Landscape Magazine*. His books include *Landscapes, American Space*, and *The Necessity of Ruins*. He has taught and lectured widely including lectureships at the University of Texas, the University of California at Berkeley, and Harvard University.

Richard Lingeman's experiences vary widely from the military to the Peace Corps. He has contributed to a broad spectrum of publications including *Madamoiselle* and the *New York Times Book Review*. He is currently editor of *The Nation*. His book, *Small Town America, A Narrative History 1620–The Present*, has made a major contribution to the field of small town studies. He has lectured widely about the American Small Town, its origins and its meanings.

David Szczerbacki is currently completing his dissertation within the Ph.D. Program, Center for Policy Studies, School of Management at the State University of New York in Buffalo. He also serves as the Economic Development Coordinator for the Southern Tier West Regional Planning and Development Board in Salamanca, New York.

Robert E. Tournier is an Associate Professor and Chairman of the Department of Psychology at the College of Charleston. He has lectured widely in the areas of historic perservation, neighborhood and urban settlement, and small towns. He has contributed articles to various journals including *Housing and Society, The Journal of Studies on Alcohol, South Atlantic Urban Studies,* and *Lifelines* and has contributed chapters to *Drug Problems of the 70's, Solutions for the 80's* and *Back to the City: Issues in Neighborhood Renovation.*